The Alchemy of Culture

RICHARD RUDGLEY

· · · · · · ·

The Alchemy of Culture

Intoxicants in Society

British Museum Press

To Robin

WARNING TO READERS

This book is not intended as a practical manual for the use of intoxicating substances. Details of certain plant preparations have been omitted to prevent its use as such.

Published by British Museum Press
A division of British Museum Publications Ltd
46 Bloomsbury Street
London WC1B 3QQ

British Library Cataloguing in Publication Data
A catalogue record for this book is available from the British Library

ISBN 0–7141–1736–6

Designed by John Hawkins

Filmset by Selwood Systems, Midsomer Norton
Printed and bound in Great Britain by
Butler & Tanner Ltd, Frome and London

Frontispiece Black stone pipe bowl in the shape of a human head facing a recumbent woman. Probably Pawnee, about 1850. London, Museum of Mankind, Bragge Collection.

Contents

· · · · · · ·

Acknowledgements   6

Introduction   7

1   Stone Age Alchemy   11

2   Frozen Tombs and Fly-Agaric Men   34

3   The Mystery of Haoma   43

4   American Dreams   56

5   The Alchemists of Afek   82

6   Lucifer's Garden   90

7   Stimulating Society   115

Conclusion   144

Notes   147

Bibliography   150

Illustration Acknowledgements   157

Index   158

Acknowledgements

· · · · · · ·

I would like to thank all those who have made this book possible, in particular Professor Alexander Piatigorsky, Dr Tadeusz Skorupski and Dr Philip Kreyenbroek for teaching me much of what I know of the ancient religious history of Asia; Dr Andrew Sherratt for his constant encouragement and enthusiasm as well as his guidance in prehistoric matters; David W. Parry for his diligent reading of the text and numerous helpful suggestions, many of which I have incorporated into the book, and above all for his friendship; and Richard Hanson of the Balfour Library, Oxford, Mike O'Hanlon and Jim Hamill of the Museum of Mankind and Ian McOmish, archivist of the Dunhill collection, for their generous assistance in locating books and photographs.

I would also like to thank everybody at British Museum Press for providing me with the opportunity to write this book. I am particularly grateful to Celia Clear, Alasdair Macleod, Liz Edwards and Teresa Francis for their patience and support.

Last, but by no means least, I would especially like to thank my father, Richard F. Rudgley, for help with points of pharmacology; I am also deeply grateful to him and to Winifred Rudgley for their hospitality and selfless giving of their time. Robin Chapman, in addition to typing the manuscript, has been the source of continual inspiration, and in thanks I dedicate this book to her.

Introduction
· · · · · · ·

These [intoxicating] substances have formed a bond of union
between men of opposite hemispheres, the uncivilised and the
civilised; they have forced passages which, once open, proved of
use for other purposes; they produced in ancient races
characteristics which have endured to the present day, evidencing
the marvellous degree of intercourse that existed between
different peoples just as certainly and exactly as a chemist can
judge the relations of two substances by their reactions.
Hundreds or thousands of years were necessary to establish
contact between whole nations by these means. Ethnology, which
should endeavour to trace their routes, has never attempted to
search out and investigate the elements of these questions, which
are of equal importance to science and to the history of mankind.

Louis Lewin, *Phantastica*

The universal human need for liberation from the restrictions of mundane
existence is satisfied by experiencing altered states of consciousness. That
we dream every night – whether we remember it or not – shows that we
have a natural predisposition to these altered states, but people also pursue
them in more active ways. Some follow the paths of prayer or meditation in
their quest for spiritual insight, whilst others are transported to the higher
planes by way of ecstasies induced by art, music, sexual passion or intoxicating substances.

In this book intoxicants are defined as those substances which alter the
state of consciousness. The possible alternatives to this term, drugs and
narcotics, are generally avoided because of their potentially negative connotations. Intoxicants and the psychoactive plants from which they derive
can be classified according to the type of altered state of consciousness which
they induce. The most useful such classification, based on that developed
by the German toxicologist Louis Lewin and revised by William Emboden,

author of the classic botanical survey *Narcotic Plants*, is as follows:

Hallucinogens: substances causing visual, auditory and other hallucinations. This class includes a variety of mushrooms, *Amanita muscaria* (the fly-agaric toadstool) and species of *Psilocybe* among them, the peyote cactus, belladonna, henbane, cannabis, harmel, LSD, mescaline, harmaline and a number of rare plants found in the Amazon Basin including species of *Banisteriopsis, Virola* and *Anadenanthera*.

Inebriants: substances causing inebriation, especially alcohol but also chloroform, ether, benzine and other solvents and volatile chemicals.

Hypnotics: substances causing states of sleep, stupor or calm, such as the mandrake, kava,[1] tranquillisers and narcotics, including opium and its derivatives (e.g. heroin).

Stimulants: substances causing an increase in mental and/or physical stimulation not usually impairing the user's performance of daily tasks. This class includes tea, coffee, cocoa, coca, cola, qat, pituri, betel, tobacco, cocaine and amphetamines. Although some mild stimulants are not strictly intoxicants, they are nevertheless included here because they have an important social role akin to that of stronger substances.

In some cases there is an overlap in the effects of a particular intoxicant. A substance classified as a stimulant may, at the end of the altered state of consciousness it induces, cause sleep, whilst a solvent (such as glue), classified here as an inebriant, may have hallucinogenic properties. Thus the four classes outlined above are not to be taken as totally distinct but rather as a general guide to the complex nature of intoxicating experiences.

In this book details of the botanical and chemical nature of intoxicating plants, such as their geographical distribution, scientific and local names[2] and psychoactive constituents, are considered in relation to the cultural aspects of preparation and consumption. These in turn are set in the wider social context in which they take place. Political, legal, economic, religious and ceremonial life all shape the way in which intoxicants are used. Special attention is given to their relationship with the art and technology of the societies in question.

One of the aims of anthropology is to understand the self by way of the other. This means that the study of other cultures can shed light on the nature of our own. Things that we take for granted about our own customs and beliefs can be seen from a fresh perspective when compared and con-

1 Nineteenth-century French print depicting the hallucinogenic effects of the inebriant ether. From G. L. Figuier, *Les Merveilles de la Science* (1867–70).

trasted with others. This book sets out to give such a perspective on the use of intoxicants in the Western world. The information that has been collected from prehistoric burial sites, tribal rituals and ancient texts may seem remote from our own world of cafés, cigarette kiosks and bars, but this circuitous route via the cultures of different times and places will lead back to ourselves and contribute to a greater understanding of aspects of our own second nature, that is to say, our culture. For such an investigation there can be no better place to start than by returning to the roots of European civilisation. Prehistoric communities laid the foundation stone upon which our culture is built, and archaeological evidence points to the important role that intoxicants played in shaping the beginnings of history.

One

. . . .

Stone Age Alchemy

The stone which the builders rejected, has been made the *headstone*
of the corner, on which rests the whole structure of the building;
but which is a stumbling-block and stone of shame, against which
they dash themselves to their ruin.

Amyraut quoted in Fulcanelli, Le Mystère des Cathédrales

The prehistoric and the 'primitive'

Prehistoric man and those people called primitive, those once termed 'the
lower races', were, in the theories of the nineteenth century, the despised
Stone Age cultures, those rejected from the edifice of 'civilisation'. Yet,
paradoxically, they became the foundation stone upon which evolutionary
theories were built. The armchair theorists of this time happily classified the
peoples of the world by a few arbitrary skull measurements and, drawing
on observations of the apparent poverty of technology, they concluded that
a corresponding paucity of culture and intelligence was the lot of these
indigenous populations. That these peoples were sophisticated enough to
be able to identify psychoactive plants and develop techniques to prepare
them for use would have been inconceivable to most scholars of the time.

J. G. Frazer, whose monumental work *The Golden Bough* (1890) is still
perhaps one of the most widely read works of anthropology, saw the
development of human consciousness as consisting of three successive
stages – from magic to religion and then to science. Those living cultures
which appeared to Frazer to be mentally enslaved to the 'bastard science' of
magic were thus conflated with prehistoric societies, the former representing
survivals of primordial states of consciousness. The general beliefs prevalent
in this primitive phase of anthropological thought were that the 'savage'
was either in the grip of a superstitious fear of supernatural entities or so

engrossed in the brute struggle for survival that his reflective capacities barely rose above those of the beasts that he stalked. Frazer, a true ivory-tower scholar, is reliably reported to have said, when asked about natives that he had actually known: 'But Heaven forbid!'. Under the assault of an ever-growing body of empirical data contradicting the grand theories of Frazer and his kind, over-speculative guesswork gave way to the meticulous investigation of other cultures that characterises modern anthropology. Pre-conceived prejudice was no longer an acceptable substitute for fact, and this more informed approach was to present both prehistoric and modern tribal societies in a more positive light. As I shall demonstrate, certain analogies can be made between the two, but this does not mean that tribal peoples live in the past nor that prehistoric man was the lumbering oaf so often portrayed.

By the Later Old Stone Age (the Upper Palaeolithic period, beginning about 45,000 to 38,000 years ago and ending around 10,000 years ago in Europe – perhaps earlier elsewhere) our species *Homo sapiens sapiens* had firmly established itself with an economy based on hunting, fishing and the gathering of plants. Some contemporary cultures practise a similar way of life and until recently it was presumed that nearly all their waking hours were spent in a relentless quest for food. In fact case-studies from various parts of the world show that sufficient food can be obtained in an average adult working day of 3–5 hours.[1] The hunter hunted by starvation may be the exception rather than the rule. The leisure time of many hunter-gatherers seems to be abundant:

> Extrapolating from ethnography to prehistory, one may say as much for the neolithic [New Stone Age] as John Stuart Mill said of all labour-saving devices, that never was one invented that saved anyone a minute's labour. The neolithic saw no particular improvement over the palaeolithic in the amount of time required per capita for the production of subsistence; probably, with the advent of agriculture, people had to work harder.[2]

Much the same conclusion is arrived at by an eminent prehistoric archaeologist:

> There is abundant data which suggests not only that hunter-gatherers have adequate supplies of food but also that they enjoy quantities of leisure time, much more in fact than do modern industrial or farm workers, or even professors of archaeology.[3]

From the basis of a comparatively stable economy and adequate leisure time Palaeolithic populations were able to develop technology, science and art to a surprisingly high degree. Prehistoric thought, albeit different in scale and content from our own, deserves our admiration. Long before even the most archaic period of metalworking there were lithic technologies producing a wide range of stone tool-kits. Prehistorians who have replicated such stone implements have clearly demonstrated that forethought is integral to the process of production. The achievements of Palaeolithic people are truly Promethean, for not only did they learn to control fire but they also laid the foundations of human art and craft. Therefore it is from the beginnings of our species that we should seek the basis of civilisation, not, as is still so often the case, from arbitrary starting-points such as Greece, Egypt or Mesopotamia.

Yet Stone Age people were not merely concerned with directly practical ventures such as tool-making and the domestication of fire. Archaeo-astronomy shows us the considerable knowledge of the skies acquired by some Neolithic communities, and, if Alexander Marshack is correct in ident-ifying markings on earlier stone and bone artefacts as references to Palaeo-lithic lunar observations, then this aspect of science can be pushed even further back in time. And prehistoric man transcended the operational level of existence in other areas too, as a world authority on Palaeolithic cave art attests:

> If technical gesture is considered as a function parallel to the function
> of concrete language, among the activities possible for the hand it is
> the activities of artistic creation that would be the indirect evidence of
> the development of abstract language.[4]

Similarly, the supposed inability of some contemporary peoples to think in an abstract fashion is the very first of many Western myths to be refuted by Lévi-Strauss in his *La Pensée Sauvage* (translated into English as *The Savage Mind*):

> [The] thirst for objective knowledge is one of the most neglected
> aspects of the thought of people we call 'primitive'. Even if it is rarely
> directed towards facts of the same level as those with which modern
> science is concerned, it implies comparable intellectual application
> and methods of observation. In both cases the universe is an object of
> thought at least as much as it is a means of satisfying needs.[5]

Almost all hunter-gatherer societies have been shown to have a fairly clear-cut division of labour between the sexes. The men hunt whilst the women gather plants and collect or hunt small animals (e.g. shellfish, birds, eggs, etc.). Whilst animal proteins are highly prized, the bulk of the staple foodstuffs are usually the result of female labour. This division of labour may suggest that in prehistoric times women's role vis-à-vis plants was not limited to the culinary or even the medical spheres, but extended into the discovery of psychoactive plants (this has a distant echo in the female-dominated European witchcraft tradition, for which see Chapter 6 below). Gatherers have an extremely detailed knowledge of their land and its natural resources, and having considered the technical and intellectual achievements of hunter-gatherer communities past and present we should not be surprised that they were able to identify, collect and process a variety of psychoactive species. R. G. Wasson, in discussing the antiquity of the use of the hallucinogenic mushroom fly-agaric, demonstrates how likely such knowledge would have been among prehistoric peoples:

> There is no reason to suppose that the peculiar virtue of this miraculous herb went for long undiscovered after it became common in the birch and pine forests as these spread over the Siberian plains in pursuit of the retreating ice cap of the last glacial age, *c.* 10,000 BC. After all, the first inhabitants probing the northlands were food gatherers, and how could they fail to see this spectacular plant with its solar disk growing around the base of the noble birch? And given their mental equipment and physical appetites, how could they fail to discover and then to take advantage of its inebriating qualities?[6]

Psychedelic art in prehistory

> At Lascaux I really believed they had come very close to an alphabet.
>
> Leroi-Gourhan, *The Dawn of European Art*

> They made words; they placed stone upon stone, they coupled these syllables of granite ... sometimes even, where there was plenty of stone and vast coast, they wrote a phrase. The immense pile of Karnac is a complete sentence.
>
> Victor Hugo, *Notre-Dame de Paris*

The foregoing section has shown that prehistoric human populations had all the faculties necessary to discover and use psychoactive plants. Yet, owing to the immense time-span being dealt with, one is still in the realm of circumstantial evidence when trying to press the case for the use of intoxicants in this archaic period. It is in prehistoric art that we may find clues to the inner life of Stone Age peoples and to the role that intoxicants may have played in it.

Although all that remains of the artistic enterprises of the Upper Palaeolithic is rock art and some small decorated objects of durable materials such as stone and bone, there is every reason to think that prehistoric man also embellished perishable materials (tents and other dwellings, wood, skin and other organics). It must be borne in mind when trying to decipher the meaning of the surviving art that we are glimpsing only certain aspects of a wider social life which is lost to us through the ravages of time. Yet the remaining fragments of this lost tradition – particularly the cave painting – bear witness to the flourishing artistic traditions of the period.

Researchers of Upper Palaeolithic art usually divide it (conveniently, if somewhat artificially) into two types – parietal art and mobile art. Parietal art literally means art found on walls, although in practice it also includes the decoration of the ceilings and floors of rock shelters and caves. The term mobile art covers a variety of portable objects (spear-throwers, 'Venus' clay figurines and other decorated artefacts). Most research has concentrated on the parietal art found in the caves of the Franco-Cantabrian area of southern France and northern Spain. Among the reasons for this emphasis are, first, the abundance of sites in this region and their geographical location, which makes them easily accessible to the French scholars who have traditionally been at the forefront of research into parietal art (most significant finds of mobile art have been in central and eastern Europe); and, secondly, the fact that the cave paintings – unlike many mobile art objects – are in their original setting, making the reconstruction of their cultural context an easier task. The sheer scale and dramatic effect of these magnificent works ensures that this emphasis will continue.

In France the Ministry of Culture officially recognises over 130 sites of Palaeolithic parietal art. Among the most spectacular are Lascaux in the Dordogne, which includes about 600 paintings and nearly 1,500 engravings, and the Grotte des Trois Frères in the French Pyrenees, where over 1,000 figures are depicted. The cave paintings consist mainly of animals and geometrical signs of uncertain meaning. The art of the whole Upper Palaeolithic period, from the Perigordian culture (beginning around 34,000 years ago) to the Magdalenian (ending about 13,000 years ago), consists of these two aspects of figurative depictions of animals and abstract signs, side by side. This reaffirms the point already made, that abstract representation (and thinking) did not evolve out of naturalistic depiction and practical thinking, but rather coexisted with it.

Statistical analysis of the animals portrayed in the Franco-Cantabrian caves has shown that carnivores are almost entirely absent. The vast majority of figures are of herbivorous species that were potential sources of food. Comparisons with photographs of animal corpses have shown that most of the painted animals are depicted in postures suggesting that they are already dead. Only a few of the images are of young animals or small mammals. We would be wrong, however, to conclude that the naturalistic aspect of the cave paintings is simply a catalogue of prehistoric diet as such. There are strange omissions from these archaic bestiaries. Leroi-Gourhan has noted that in the whole of the Lascaux complex only one reindeer is depicted, whilst the large quantity of reindeer bones among the debris found on the floor of the cave indicates that it was a major source of food in the Ice Age. Such anomalies are difficult to explain.

In order to try and understand why certain animals and not others were depicted in the paintings, prehistorians have resorted to the methods of ethnographic analogy and have attempted to shed light on the practices of ancient hunters by analysing reports on the behaviour of modern hunter-gatherers studied by anthropologists. Salomon Reinach was one of the first to draw on the ideas of hunting magic outlined by Frazer and other early anthropologists. He saw cave art as a form of sympathetic magic whereby prehistoric man sought to attract game and bring success in hunting by painting his prey. More recently Steven Mithen has updated this hunting magic thesis by suggesting that the art was a medium for the storage and transmission of information on hunting, a kind of blackboard which experienced hunters would use to teach young men about the movement of game and other aspects of animal behaviour. However, there are problems with this interpretation which arise out of the very ethnographic analogies that are marshalled to support it. Evidence shows that in both African and Australian hunter-gatherer societies such things as animal migration, tracks and dung are studied first-hand by youths accompanying older men on hunting trips, seemingly precluding a need for a prehistoric classroom separated from the 'hands-on' business of hunting. To be fair to Mithen, he does not claim his information gathering theory to be the one and only explanation of Palaeolithic art. Up until the 1960s almost all the interpretations of the paintings suffered from a common fault, namely the assumption that they had a single purpose. There may have been a host of reasons why Palaeolithic people chose to decorate these sites, and more recently interpreters of their art have, on the whole, rejected the possibility of finding a skeleton key to unlock all the secrets of the caves.

If it is difficult to interpret the figures of animals in Palaeolithic art, the geometric signs present even greater problems. There are those who see these simple shapes as directly referring to tangible objects such as dwellings or nets and traps for catching animals. Mithen expands his thesis on the meaning of the figurative art to include some of these so-called abstract signs. He claims some of these images are not abstract signs at all but representations of tracks and prints. Among the examples he cites to prove his point are an engraved bison and a depiction of a horse: these figures, from separate sites, are both superimposed by what were thought to be abstract motifs but are, he argues, the hoofprints of the respective animals. In such cases his interpretation is persuasive, but many other signs still remain beyond such naturalistic explanations. The dark, wet and inhospitable caves were, we know, not generally used as dwellings. Yet the very scale of the art suggests that they were sacred sites, perhaps used for rituals, initiations and visionary quests by prehistoric shamans. The purpose of these spectacular sanctuaries is as obscure as the hieroglyphic language of the strange signs accompanying the portrayal of animals. Ethnographic analogies, whilst suggestive, cannot alone provide us with a full understanding of them.

In an attempt to explain the signs David Lewis-Williams has dug down beneath cultural comparisons into the bedrock of the workings of the human nervous system, where he believes these images have their origin. His explanation was outlined in an article co-written with Thomas Dowson, a colleague from the Rock Art Research Unit of the University of Witwatersrand in South Africa, and published in 1988. The authors begin by noting that:

> Under certain circumstances the visual system generates a range of luminous percepts that are independent of light from an external source ... because they derive from the human nervous system, all people who enter certain altered states of consciousness (ASC), no matter what their cultural background, are liable to perceive them. These geometric visual percepts can be induced by a variety of means. Under laboratory conditions, electrical stimulation and flickering light produce them, but, although flickering fire light may have played a

role in the past, we clearly have to look elsewhere to explain prehistoric experience. Psychoactive drugs generate the percepts, but fatigue, sensory deprivation, intense concentration, auditory driving, migraine, schizophrenia, hyperventilation, and rhythmic movement are some other generating factors.[7]

These visual percepts are sometimes called phosphenes or form constants, but the authors include them under the generic term entoptic phenomena. There are a number of entoptic forms, but the article is concerned with six basic ones. They are (i) a basic grid sometimes expanding into a lattice or hexagonal pattern, (ii) sets of parallel lines, (iii) dots or short flecks, (iv) zigzag lines (angular or undulating), (v) nested curves, and (vi) filigrees or meandering lines. These basic entoptic forms may be perceived by the subject in a variety of ways. For example, the form may be fragmentary or it may be merged with another form to build up a more complex geometric image. The altered states of consciousness that induce entoptic phenomena and hallucinatory visions consist, it is said, of three stages. In the initial stage entoptic images appear alone and cannot be controlled consciously. This gives way to a second, more elaborate, stage in which the subject embellishes the entoptic form with some iconic significance (e.g. a zigzag line may be interpreted as a snake or as lightning). In the final stage there is a shift of emphasis away from entoptic forms and toward more hallucinatory iconic imagery.

The sequence of three stages was first established by laboratory research using LSD and mescaline. Whilst admitting that this model may not adequately represent all altered states of consciousness induced either by intoxicants or other means, Lewis-Williams and Dowson nevertheless believe it to describe a wide range of such experiences. They cite Gerardo Reichel-Dolmatoff's work on intoxicant use among the Tukano Indians of the Amazon (for a detailed discussion of the Tukano, see pp. 59–68 below) as supporting the widespread applicability of the model. Tukano experiences are said to correspond with the findings in the laboratory, both in the perception of entoptic forms and in their occurrence in three stages.

Two distinct types of images are thus perceived – geometric entoptic images deriving from the universal human nervous system (the neurologically controlled elements) and hallucinatory iconic images deriving from the subject's mind or culture (the psychological and cultural elements). The writers then proceed to investigate two ethnographic examples of rock art to see if they can identify this neuropsychological model in the anthropological evidence. It is significant for our purpose to note that both the cultures in question (the San bushmen of the Kalahari Desert and the Shoshonean Coso of the California Great Basin) appear to have used intoxicants to obtain their visions. In both cases they seem to have left a visual record of their spiritual journeys in the form of rock art. Fig. 2 shows that entoptic images played a role in both San and Coso rock art, and this leads the authors to suggest that the comparable geometric signs of Upper Palaeolithic art are, in fact, entoptic images produced in an altered state of consciousness. The various ways of generating entoptic phenomena outlined above (sensory deprivation, fatigue, illness etc.) are paralleled in shamanic vision quests. Mircea Eliade, in his well-known monograph on shamanism, lists a variety of states that precipitate spiritual journeys. Among them are physical illness, nervous disorders of a temporary kind, dancing and drumming to the point of exhaustion, and ritual solitude in caves and other isolated sites. Lewis-Williams and Dowson suggest that the painted caves of western Europe, being both removed from daily prehistoric life and difficult of access, would have provided an ideal location for initiatory and shamanic visions.

So, have Lewis-Williams and his colleague deciphered the language of these Stone Age signs? Among critics there are those who despair of ever understanding the signs, whilst others prefer alternative explanations (e.g. that the marks represent naturalistic objects or are just meaningless doodles). Whilst a few of the signs can be explained by such suggestions, the majority are left undeciphered and the view that they are entoptic phenomena is both original and compelling. As I shall show in the following chapters, such images appear in hallucinatory experiences from a variety of cultural contexts and this strengthens the case for the Palaeolithic use of intoxicants.

Whilst finding the idea of entoptic phenomena relevant to prehistoric studies, Richard Bradley, a specialist in the archaeology of Neolithic Europe, believes that our lack of background knowledge of Palaeolithic cultural life makes the theory difficult to corroborate. He suggests that applying the idea to the megalithic art made by the early farmers of the Neolithic period may be a more fruitful line of research. He considers the art of two distinct regions of north-west Europe, southern Brittany *c.* 4900 BC–*c.* 3200 BC and the Boyne Valley (Ireland) and other sites of the British Isles *c.* 3400 BC–*c.* 2400 BC, both of which include geometric motifs reminiscent of the entoptic phenomena already discussed. For the present purpose I will limit my analysis to Brittany. The earlier art depicted on the Breton megaliths is largely naturalistic and represents themes linking population, land and food supply. Depictions of axes, bows and arrows and cattle, as well as images resembling either hafted axes or ploughs, and perhaps shepherds' crooks, are all common

ENTOPTIC PHENOMENA			SAN ROCK ART	
			ENGRAVINGS	PAINTINGS
	A	B	C	D
I				
II				
III				
IV				
V				
VI				

2 Entoptic images found in San and Coso rock art, compared with geometric signs in Upper Palaeolithic art. After Lewis-Williams and Dowson 1988, 206–7.

motifs and seem to mirror the changes in lifestyle that accompanied the development of farming in the region. The axe symbols seem to reflect the importance of clearing the land and the depiction of cattle the increasing emphasis on livestock.

The monuments of the latter part of the period became more complex,

COSO	PALAEOLITHIC ART			
	MOBILE ART		PARIETAL ART	
E	Γ	G	H	I

the tomb chambers became larger and in some cases contained separate compartments and side cells. The naturalistic representations of the earlier phase continued to be used but were accompanied by geometric motifs such as spirals, parallel curving lines and nested arcs. Most of this art has been found inside the tombs, cut off from the light of day – just like the earlier

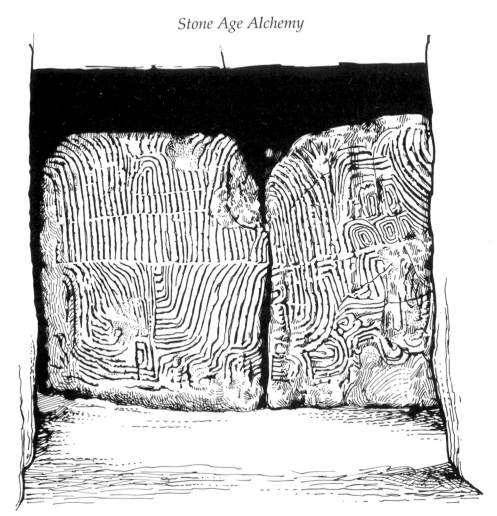

3 Carved stones from the Neolithic tomb of Gavrinis in Brittany.

Palaeolithic cave-sanctuaries. The need for artificial lighting coupled with the sacred nature of such places would have made the megaliths ideal sites for inducing trance states that would have included the perception of entoptic phenomena, as Bradley hints may have been the case. A particularly dramatic example of this psychedelic art is the decorated tomb of Gavrinis, an island in the Gulf of Morbihan, where geometric motifs are elaborated into complex patterns (see fig. 3).

But is there any evidence that this art was inspired by psychoactive drugs rather than by the other methods of inducing trance and hallucinatory experiences alluded to in my discussion of the Palaeolithic period? In the early fourth millennium BC a new and distinctive type of artefact appeared in the archaeological record of Middle Neolithic France. Often called 'vase-supports', these objects in fact appear to be braziers, as some have traces of burning on them. They are small, shallow, bowl-like containers set in a cylindrical or cubic stand (see fig. 4). That they are usually highly decorated suggests that their use was more than mundane. The distribution of these braziers throughout the various cultural regions of Neolithic France indicates that, rather than being a local innovation, they announce the arrival of a new cultural trait. They seem to have diffused from south to north, and have been unearthed in the caves of southern France, in ritual enclosures in the Paris Basin and, interestingly, at the megalithic sites of Brittany. Approximately 160 have been found within a cromlech (enclosure of standing stones) at the sacred site of Er Lannic, an island facing the passage grave of Gavrinis, site of the psychedelic images discussed above. Andrew Sherratt

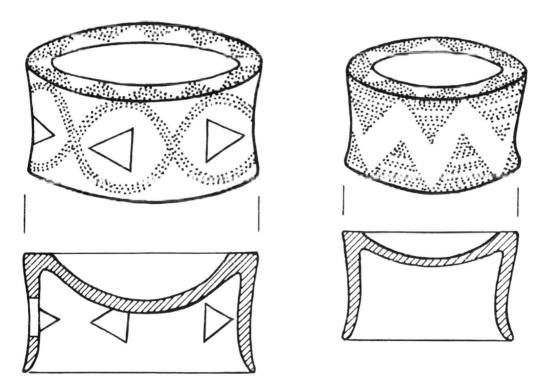

4 Pottery 'vase-supports', probably used for burning opium, from the ceremonial site of Er Lannic, Brittany. From Sherratt 1991, fig. 2.

23

has suggested that these braziers may have been used for the ritual burning of opium in the Neolithic sanctuaries:

> Is it a coincidence that the appearance of the apparatus of a southern cult should occur in northern France at the same time as Breton megalithic art reached its climax in the complex forms of the Gavrinis carvings, recently interpreted as entoptic images produced under the influence of drugs? Since the palaeobotanical evidence suggests a west Mediterranean focus for the use of *Papaver somniferum*, this would seem to constitute a *prima facie* case for the ritual use of opium as a narcotic.[8]

It is, of course, possible that the braziers were used to burn other, non-intoxicating, substances; but opium use in such contexts is a strong possibility for, as I shall demonstrate, the poppy was well known to the Neolithic farmer.

Opium and hemp

The opium poppy (*Papaver somniferum*) – not to be confused with the red or common poppy (*Papaver rhoeas*) – is an annual herb cultivated widely in various temperate and sub-tropical regions. It is one of the most important medical plants known to man and contains many narcotic alkaloids (including morphine, codeine, papaverine, narceine, thebaine and narcotine). Opium is the congealed latex deriving from the sap of the unripe capsule of the poppy. It is extracted by cutting fine slits into the outer surface of the capsule and collecting the exuded juice the following day. The latex is then formed into lumps and dried in the shade. Despite the exhaustive surveys of Merlin, Krikorian and other experts, the taxonomy, geographical origins and early cultural uses of the opium poppy remain uncertain. It seems, however, that it was domesticated in the west Mediterranean area possibly as far back as the sixth millennium BC. Most of the palaeobotanical evidence for the prehistoric use of the opium poppy comes from sites in west central Europe. As early as 1878 seeds were discovered at the sites of Neolithic lake villages in Switzerland; the same country has yielded at least seventeen separate finds from the Neolithic period and a further ten from the Bronze Age, which suggests a stable and continuous tradition of cultivation. Similar finds from Germany and Italy demonstrate the widespread domestication of the plant from Neolithic times. The presence of seeds at Iron Age sites in southern England and in Poland indicates the expansion of the species was from south to north. This is, of course, compatible with Sherratt's suggestion that the cultic use of opium as an intoxicant was imported from the south. However, the seeds themselves do not contain opium and were probably used in baking, as they still are today. The oil that can be extracted from the seeds is reported to be similar to olive oil and thus could have been used both for cooking and as a lamp fuel.

Although we may infer that, since the opium poppy was well known in Neolithic communities its intoxicating properties were not likely to have remained unknown, more substantial evidence is required to establish this beyond reasonable doubt. Such evidence is now available, due to discoveries made at a burial cave at Albuñol near the coast of Granada in southern Spain. This site, the Cueva de los Murciélagos (i.e. 'Bat Cave', so called on account of the large deposits of bat droppings found there), was explored in the mid-nineteenth century and the finds were subsequently published by Góngora y Martinez. They have recently been re-studied by the archaeologist C. A. Giner and radiocarbon dated to *c.* 4200 BC. Many of the burials were accompanied by globular bags of esparto grass (*Stipa tenacissima*) and among the items found within these bags were a considerable number of opium poppy capsules. These particular finds indicate that not only did the opium poppy play an important role amongst the communities that deposited their dead in the cave, but that it was probably used as an intoxicant.

That opium played an important role in the Bronze Age of the east Mediterranean has been demonstrated by analysis of Cypriot Bronze Age pots discovered in Egypt. Among the vessels described in the literature as Cypriote Base-Ring I ware are three basic types – the juglet, the bottle and the flask – all dating from the Eighteenth Dynasty in Egypt (New Kingdom period). A later set of pottery types, Base-Ring II ware, were also imported into Egypt from Cyprus (most of them have been found in Tell el-Amarna, the city of Akhenaten). The juglet was the most common import of all the types. Why this was so must have been for one or more of the following reasons: for its ornamental function, for its intrinsic usefulness or for its contents. Whilst the first two reasons may have been contributing factors to the extensive importing of the juglets, it is the contents which explain their economic value. We know that the narrow necks of the juglets point to liquid contents, as solid substances could not have been emptied through such small apertures. Working along a line of highly innovative thinking, Robert Merrillees has argued that the Cypriote export merchants of the Bronze Age could have best announced the nature of their product by designing a vessel whose shape would easily communicate the nature of its contents. That many of their foreign customers would not have understood any written language except their own, while others would have been altogether illiterate, makes this the most viable method of advertising their wares. Even in our own society such strategies in packaging may be found:

> Today, when literacy in this country, for example, might be thought to have made such measures unnecessary, we have only to look through our cupboards to find objects which make analogies with Bronze Age usage irresistible. Who could mistake the nature of the contents inside a plastic vessel shaped like a lemon or a tomato?[9]

So, what are the juglets supposed to advertise? It is common in the archaeological analysis of pottery to look for metal or leather vessels which have been imitated in the ceramic productions of a community. Such borrowings of shape from one material to another are known as skeuomorphs. But, in the case of the juglet, it is not to some original in metal or leather that we must look, but to the head of the opium poppy. The undeniable similarity of shape between the poppy capsule and the Base-Ring I juglet is shown in fig. 5. The base-ring of the pot spreads out in imitation of the stigma on top of the poppy capsule (which is drawn upside down), whilst the long, thin neck of the juglet parallels the stalk of the poppy. The funnel rim of the juglet is probably a feature designed to facilitate easy pouring of the contents and does not correspond to any feature of the poppy. That the Base-Ring juglet is a skeuomorph of the poppy capsule indicates the contents were probably an infusion of opium. Merrillees' thesis has since been vindicated by the findings of the biochemist John Evans of the North-East London Polytechnic (now University). His analysis of organic residues on Cypriote Base-Ring pottery (using up-to-date techniques in chromatography and spectroscopy) shows that opium was indeed present in at least some of the juglets.

The role of opium in the ancient world is well attested. There are references to it in writings from Egypt, Assyria and Greece. Egyptian medical texts list among opium's many uses its sedative powers to alleviate the pain of wounds, abscesses and scalp complaints. For the Romans too it was something of a panacea, being used to treat elephantiasis, carbuncles, liver complaints, epilepsy and scorpion bites, according to Pliny (*Natural History,* Book XX). But are we to think that those Egyptian customers of the Cypriote opium merchants used the contents of the juglets solely for medical purposes? Merrillees thinks not:

5 *Left*: Base-ring I juglet from Egypt, Eighteenth Dynasty, *c.* 1550–1295 BC. Petrie Museum, University College, London. *Right*: an opium poppy capsule. After Merrillees 1962, pl. XLIII.

It would be impossible to believe that advantage was not taken by the ancient Egyptians of the purely sensuous or erotic effects that opium also produces. Indeed Kritikos has shown that during the Late Minoan III period [of Cretan civilisation] opium was taken by participants in certain religious ceremonies to induce a state of ecstasy essential for the performance of the sacred rites. Might not opium have been used in the same way in Egypt? How appropriate it would be if the island of Aphrodite could be proved to have introduced Egypt to the drug which served that Goddess so well![10]

This brief survey of the use of *Papaver somniferum* indicates that opium infusions (opium is soluble in both water and wine) were imported from Bronze Age Cyprus into Egypt for medical reasons and probably also as a means of inducing altered states of consciousness – although in a secular rather than a religious context – and perhaps even as an aphrodisiac. Bearing this in mind, it seems highly unlikely that the Neolithic farmers who knew the poppy so well found no use for it beyond baking and burning its seed oil. The discovery of opium poppy capsules in the 'Bat Cave' in Spain and the braziers of Brittany and elsewhere suggest that the plant had a ceremonial function. Such an important sacred role could not have been given to the humble seed but must surely be based on the intoxicating effects of the opium itself.

A similar case can be made for the use of hemp (*Cannabis sativa*) as an intoxicant in prehistoric Europe. Hemp seeds have been found at a variety of Neolithic sites in Germany, Switzerland, Austria and Romania. Like the opium poppy, hemp grows as a weed, and its proximity to prehistoric communities was a factor in its domestication. The rubbish piles that existed around Neolithic settlements, being rich in organic nitrogen, would have been ideal sites for the growth of nitrophiles (nitrogen-loving plants) such as hemp. It was probably in such locations that the plant first became known to those communities who later cultivated it.

Although hemp may have been cultivated for a variety of purposes – for instance its fatty, rather poor-quality seed oil – its primary practical use was, and still is, its fibre[11] (for a detailed account of the uses of this versatile fibre see Boyce 1900). In the Neolithic its fibre could have been used in the making of coarse textiles, cordage and sacking, and it seems likely that it had another important role in prehistory, namely as an intoxicant. In several parts of eastern Europe decorated pottery objects called polypod bowls have been found, dating from the early third millennium BC (see fig. 6). The earliest of these bowls, often interpreted as braziers, came from the Pontic Steppes. Examples found in the Carpathian Basin and then in Czechoslovakia and southern Germany are somewhat later, indicating that this type of pottery spread from east to west. *Cannabis sativa*, too, is generally thought to have originated on the steppes and subsequently to have spread into Europe. Could it be that these polypod bowls, rather like the earlier 'vase-supports', were braziers for the ritual burning of an intoxicant? Two further finds of associated artefacts add weight to the possibility of a later Neolithic cannabis cult. A pit-grave (*kurgan*) burial of the later third millennium in Romania was discovered to include an item described as a 'pipe cup' which itself

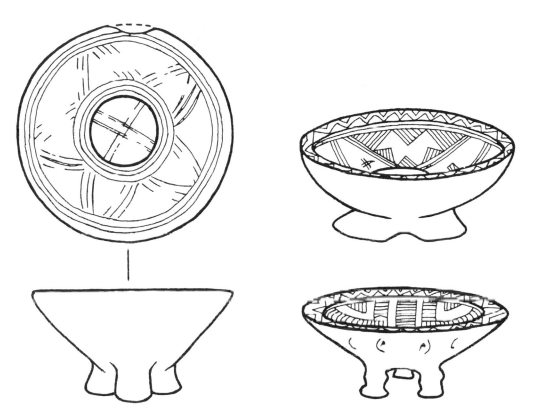

6 Pottery polypod bowls from eastern and central Europe, probably used for burning hemp. From Sherratt 1991, fig. 3.

contained charred hemp seeds. Another 'pipe cup' from the same period and belonging to the north Caucasian Early Bronze Age was found with hemp seed present. Although the seeds are not themselves psychoactive, they are the most heat-resistant part of the plant, and these two finds suggest that the intoxicating flowers and leaves had been burnt away.

Contemporary with the rise of the polypod bowls on the steppe was the development of a novel style of pottery ornamentation. While the bowl was still wet, cord was wrapped around it in order to impress it with a pattern. Taking a leaf out of Merrillees' book, Sherratt has suggested that this cord decoration may have been a way of celebrating the contents of the bowls. In this case it was not by imitating the shape of the *Cannabis sativa* plant (as the Cypriote juglets imitated the opium poppy) that the contents of the vessels were announced, but by decoration applied by the use of hemp cord. Both the fibre and intoxicating qualities of hemp were exploited by later cultures such as the Thracians. A Greek source informs us that they made their garments from its fibre[12] and it is known that their shamans (*Kapnobatai*) used cannabis to induce states of trance.[13]

As the polypod bowls decorated with cord impressions began to be used further westward, they entered cultural areas with a tradition of alcohol use. It is possible that in such regions the two substances were used together to produce a new psychoactive effect. Just as it can be shown that the use of opium was widespread in the early historical period in the east Mediterranean, there is also sufficient evidence that hemp was being used as an intoxicant by the Iron Age. Cannabis has been discovered in the grave chamber of the Hochdorf Hallstatt D waggon-burial near Stuttgart in Germany (dating from about 500 BC), and also at Scythian sites on the steppes (for the use of intoxicants by the Scythians, see Chapter 2).

There are clear parallels in the use of opium and hemp in prehistoric times. Both grew as weeds near human habitations and are known to have been domesticated in the Neolithic as multi-purpose plants. In both cases distinctive ceramic braziers were probably used for the inhalation of the smoke of the respective substances. Although it is only after the Neolithic period (when the archaeological record becomes sufficiently detailed) that we have direct and irrefutable proof that these plants were used as intoxicants, the circumstantial evidence for their use as such in the Neolithic is highly persuasive.

The rise of the drinking complex in Europe

Although fermentation, by which sugar is transformed by yeast to make alcohol, is a process which occurs naturally, it does not seem to have been exploited by the early Neolithic cultures. There are good reasons why the use of alcohol was not widespread at this time:

> All the encyclopedia entries on alcohol start by saying that it began way back in prehistory. I am not so sure. I think it is more like horses, ploughs and woolly sheep – a second generation development of the farming tradition, with its origins in the south. The sugars available to prehistoric man were glucose, fructose, maltose and lactose, available from honey, fruits, sprouting grain and milk respectively, to produce mead, wine, beer and koumish [*milchsnapps* or fermented

mare's milk]. Few of these sources of sugar were abundant in primeval temperate Europe, and our own, sugar-saturated environment is a poor guide to the conditions that obtained then. Fermentation is constantly happening accidentally now – in some long-forgotten bag of fruit in the kitchen – but only because of the highly selected, sugar-rich varieties of fruit that are now so easily available on the supermarket shelves. Wild fruits – and this includes the wild grape *Vitis sylvestris* – simply don't have enough sugar to ferment. Given that the process also includes lengthy preparation in closed containers with the appropriate variety of yeast, I think it entirely probable that alcohol was not invented in Europe.[14]

The origin of alcohol use is rather to be traced to the fourth millennium and the tree crops of the eastern Mediterranean and Mesopotamia. The earliest alcoholic beverages were probably drawn from the fruit and sap of the date palm, which is one of the most concentrated sources of naturally occurring sugar. Cultivated vines (*Vitis vinifera*) also contain sufficient sugar, as well as natural yeasts. Beer (probably barley beer) is referred to in early Sumerian and Akkadian texts, and from the Protoliterate period of Mesopotamia (*c.* 3200 BC) we find illustrations of drinking straws, needed to consume beer in which the cereal grains had not been de-husked. Egyptian figurines dating from the Predynastic period show the use of brewing vats.

It is to the Early Bronze Age cultures of the Aegean and Anatolia (Asia Minor), in the early period from 3500 to 2000 BC, that we must look for the immediate origins of the diffusion of alcohol throughout Europe. These communities consumed their wine from metal drinking vessels, and their more northerly neighbours of the Baden culture in central Europe have been shown by the archaeologist Nándor Kalicz to have echoed the design of these vessels in their own pottery (see fig. 7). Various features of Baden ceramics, such as their fluting, strap-handles and dimpled bases, clearly have their origins in the techniques used for shaping metal prototypes. The Baden culture not only lacked the necessary knowledge of sheet metalworking to make metal cups, but was also beyond the limits of viticulture, which only reached this area in Roman times. So the liquids consumed from their pottery imitations of southern metalware were also a substitute. They probably drank mead, rather than grape-wine.

Not long after this, another distinctive complex of vessels for holding liquids, known as Globular Amphorae, appeared over an area of Europe from Hamburg to Kiev. This new ceramic style was influenced both by

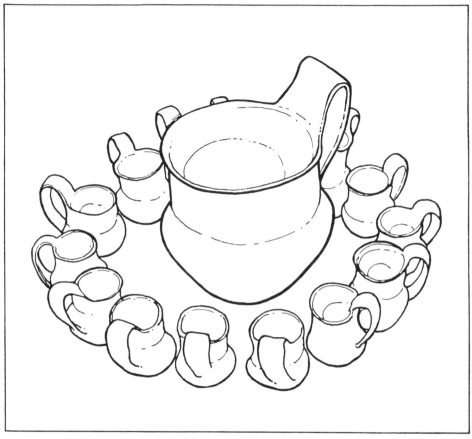

7 Pottery drinking set of the Neolithic Baden culture of central Europe, based on metal prototypes. From Sherratt 1987, fig. 9a.

Baden pottery and by the cord decoration of the steppe cultures. It is possible, on this line of argument, that their brews may have combined alcohol and *Cannabis sativa* in a potent infusion! The popularity of heavily decorated drinking vessels continued to spread further northward into central and eastern Europe with the Corded Ware Beakers. These beakers (which are large drinking cups) were decorated with rows of cord impressions; their great cultural importance is attested by the fact that they recur again and again in the burials of the period alongside two other types of distinctive male artefacts – the flint dagger and the shaft-hole stone battle-axe. The final phase (*c.* 2500–2000 BC) in the initial diffusion of vessels plausibly associated with the use of alcoholic drinks is marked by the spread of Bell Beakers, which first brought this type of drinking vessel to Britain and the Atlantic coasts and are often found in graves together with archery equipment and the first metal daggers.

The use of alcohol in later Neolithic Europe should not be separated from the overall cultural picture of which it was just a part. As Sherratt explains:

> The spread of the drinking complex – a common emphasis on sets of vessels, often combined in graves, which in several cases are so distinctive stylistically as to have given their name to whole cultures – took place during a period of unusually rapid social, cultural and economic change. During this time, Europe was opened up – both literally, in terms of the further deforestation of its landscapes, and metaphorically, in terms of its new contacts and social opportunities. Fundamental to this process was the increasing importance of livestock, and the emergence of male warrior elites whose sub culture was portrayed in the characteristic combination of weaponry and drinking vessels in their graves.[15]

Alcohol in this early phase of European life was a rarity, and in the more northerly climes various sugar-producing substances were pressed into the service of producing intoxicating brews. Organic residues from later pre-historic vessels show that cereal grains, honey and fruits were all mixed together to make a composite drink which was at once a mead, an ale and a fruit wine. The use of this new liquid intoxicant may initially have been combined with opium or hemp, but it was soon to establish itself as the primary intoxicant of Western culture, a position it still maintains.

This analysis of the prehistoric use of psychoactive substances suggests that the highly decorated Neolithic vessels were embellished in a manner appropriate to their contents and that their prominent position in the archaeological record was not due to any intrinsic worth of the pottery itself. That such substances could be directly reflected in the variety of Neolithic ceramic styles has far-reaching implications for prehistoric studies. It is through the work of those few archaeologists who have considered the often neglected topic of intoxicants that new ways of looking at the spread of cultural complexes in Europe (and, by extension, to other continents) have been developed.

Two

· · · · · · ·

Frozen Tombs and Fly-Agaric Men

The importance of the hallucinogen cannabis in the prehistoric steppe cultures continued into historical times. It was used by the shamans of the Scythian communities, especially in the context of funeral rites, yet as the masters of the steppe came under increasing Greek influence they turned to the delights of alcoholic inebriation. The steppe cultures had once introduced cannabis to Europe, but by Scythian times the main direction of the transmission of intoxicants had started to reverse. Further to the north and east the shamans of Siberia had been using the hallucinogenic fly-agaric mushroom (*Amanita muscaria*) since time immemorial. This practice continues in isolated pockets to this day, although the majority of Siberians – like the Scythians before them – eventually succumbed to the drinking complex that arrived with the European colonists.

Frozen tombs

> To Earth's far-distant confines we are come,
> The tract of Scythia, waste untrod by man.
>
> Aeschylus, *Prometheus Bound*

To the Greeks the hard-drinking, cannabis-using Scythians were barbarians living beyond the *oikumene*, or limits of civilisation. Yet these steppe dwellers were no unruly mob of brigands raiding their sedentary neighbours as and when the opportunity arose, but a highly organised confederacy of chiefdoms with their own kings holding the reins of power. The legendary horsemanship of the Scythians was the key to their military success, and the lightning attacks of the nomads struck fear into the hearts of their victims.

Frozen Tombs and Fly-Agaric Men

It is as aggressors that they first appear in the annals of history. In the eighth century BC Scythian groups from the east began to migrate westward with their flocks and herds, eventually driving another pastoral people, the Cimmerians, out of the region to the north of the Black Sea. After a successful alliance with the Medes, which resulted in the sacking of the Assyrian city of Nineveh in 613 BC, both the Asiatic and the European Scythians began a series of conflicts with the Persian kings of the Achaemenian Dynasty.

Among the tribute-bearing delegations depicted on Achaemenian reliefs at the royal site of Persepolis is a people named *saka tigraxauda*, or 'pointed-hat Scythians', on account of their distinctive headgear. Another group that features in a number of trilingual inscriptions in Old Persian, Elamite and Akkadian[1] is the *saka haumavarga* or '*haoma*-drinking Scythians'. *Haoma* was an intoxicant used among the ancient Indo-Iranian people and the controversy over its identity is the subject of Chapter 3. The name *saka haumavarga* implies that other Scythian groups did not use this particular psychoactive substance.

I have already referred to the steppe origins of the cannabis cult in Neolithic times, and the prehistoric technique of inhaling its intoxicating smoke from braziers is echoed in the practices of the Scythians. In the fifth century BC the Greek historian Herodotus travelled widely in the area to the north of the Black Sea and includes the following account of Scythian intoxication in his *Histories*:

> On a framework of tree sticks, meeting at the top, they stretch pieces of woollen cloth. Inside this tent they put a dish with hot stones on it. Then they take some hemp seed, creep into the tent, and throw the seed on the hot stones. At once it begins to smoke, giving off a vapour unsurpassed by any vapour bath one could find in Greece. The Scythians enjoy it so much they howl with pleasure.[2]

In analysing this passage some scholars have suggested that the naïve Herodotus was unaware that he was witnessing a method of intoxication and believed it was merely a more pleasurable variant of the vapour bath familiar to him from his own culture. The vapour baths of many Arctic and sub-Arctic peoples are known to serve not merely for the cleansing of the physical body but also for the purification of the spirit. A well-known example is the sweat-lodge of the American Indians in which the shaman supervises curing ceremonies. Bearing in mind these cultural analogies, there is no good reason to reject the possibility that the Scythian shamans used the ecstatic vapour bath that Herodotus describes as a purification rite.

Often dubbed the 'father of history', Herodotus has also received the less flattering epithet 'the father of lies' on account of some rather fanciful passages in his writings. But in this particular instance his accuracy was

8 Scythian copper vessels and metal tent poles, found in a burial at Pazyryk in Siberia dating from about 400 BC and used in the preparation of hemp inhalations. From Rudenko 1970, pl. 62.

dramatically vindicated by an archaeological discovery at the other end of the Scythian world. Between 1947 and 1951 the Soviet archaeologist S. I. Rudenko supervised the excavation of five large burial mounds (*kurgans*) at the site of Pazyryk in the Altai mountain region of south-east Siberia. These tombs were preserved in a remarkably good state because the shafts which had been dug to contain them flooded and, owing to the severity of the local winters, became frozen. The great pile of earth and stones which covered the burial chambers prevented any thawing taking place below ground. As a result many organic materials (such as textiles, leather and the bodies of men and horses) were preserved alongside more durable objects, giving a more complete picture of Scythian culture than could ever have been hoped for. Among the various important finds were two copper censers containing the charred remains of hemp seeds as well as the stones used to heat them and a tent frame consisting of six metal rods (see fig. 8). Not only do these discoveries prove Herodotus' accuracy as an historian, but they attest to the remarkable geographical continuity of Scythian practices, for the site of Pazyryk is thousands of miles east of the Black Sea region in which he witnessed the very same equipment in use! When considering this alongside the fact that these metal braziers are the descendants of more modest pre-historic prototypes dating back thousands of years, one must accept that cannabis played a profound role in shaping cultural life on the steppes.

Over the centuries the European Scythians became more absorbed into the spreading drinking complex and augmented their traditional intoxicant with imported Greek wine, as the discovery of seals and writing on amphorae from their well-stocked cellars shows. But old habits die hard, and even when the Scythians finally faded from history in the third century A D the cult of cannabis lived on among the nomadic groups who replaced them.

Fly-agaric men

The shaman is a religious specialist who combines the roles of doctor, priest and sorcerer in the pursuit of his or her vocation. Such individuals, who were seen to have special access to the spiritual world, were called *saman* by the Tungus people of Siberia, and this word, in its modified form, has come down to us through the early Russian accounts of Siberian life. The Siberian shamans were guardians of the traditions of their culture, and their knowledge of myths, songs, medicines and religious rites was extensive. It is reported that the vocabulary of the Yakut shamans consisted of some 12,000 words, three times that of the average member of the community.

The role of intoxicants in the shamanic traditions of North Asia has been the subject of some disagreement. Mircea Eliade, the renowned professor of the history of religions, has claimed that although mushroom intoxication produces contact with the spiritual world it does so in a 'passive and crude' way. He describes such practices as decadent, late and derivative in their attempts to imitate an earlier 'purer' form of shamanism. The spiritual journeys of these lesser shamans are achieved in a 'mechanical and corrupt' fashion. Whilst the use of tobacco and alcohol as intoxicants is a late practice (both were introduced by Russian traders and settlers), Eliade makes the mistake of conflating such intoxication with that produced by mushrooms. Here it is not Eliade's scholarly impartiality speaking, but rather his bourgeois aversion to intoxication in relation to religious life. The facts firmly refute his attempt to reconstruct the history of Siberian shamanism along such lines. As will be shown, there is no reason to doubt the antiquity of the use of hallucinogenic mushrooms among the North Eurasian peoples, and it is a matter of some concern that Eliade's book *Shamanism: Archaic Techniques of Ecstasy*, probably the most widely consulted comparative study of the shamanic complex, includes such a basic misrepresentation of the facts. This fault is compounded in his discussion of the Americas (and beyond), where shamanic intoxication is also well attested but likewise receives only superficial attention from the author.

References to the use of the hallucinogenic fly-agaric mushroom or toadstool (*Amanita muscaria*) go back to the early period of Russian contacts with

9 *Amanita muscaria*, the fly-agaric mushroom.

the Siberian peoples. The first known account is found in a journal written in 1658 by a Polish prisoner of war, who describes its use among the Ostyak of Western Siberia. The myths of many Siberian peoples contain fly-agaric themes (see below) and there is no reason to suppose that these are recent insertions. Linguistic and archaeological evidence likewise indicates the antiquity of mushroom use. In many Finno-Ugric languages words meaning 'ecstasy', 'intoxication' and 'drunkenness' are traceable to names meaning fungus or fly-agaric. Siberian cliff drawings depicting armless, one-legged figures bear a remarkable resemblance to the descriptions of 'fly-agaric men' who appear to those under the influence of *Amanita muscaria*. These have been dated to the Bronze Age by Okladnikov, and similar drawings have been documented by Dikov and others.[3]

This is not meant to give the impression that all Siberian cultures used the fly-agaric; some patently did not. But in many of those that did, the mushroom had a central and revered role in shamanic practices. Among the Vogul peoples the consumption of the fly-agaric was restricted to sacred occasions, and it was abused on peril of death. To the Ugrian shaman it was as essential to his vocation as the drum. Among the Selkup it was believed that consumption of the fly-agaric by those who were not shamans could be fatal. Only some shamans among them used it; others preferred alternative methods of achieving spiritual ecstasy.

Although there are many scattered references to the mushroom from various parts of North Asia, its use among the peoples of the Palaeosiberian (or Hyperborean) language group of Eastern Siberia is the best documented. The Chukchee, Kamchadal and Koryak belonging to this group had economies based on reindeer-herding inland and, in coastal areas, on the hunting of large sea-mammals (seals, walrus and whales). All three used the fungus in question, and it was most commonly consumed by the Koryak in whose lands it grew most abundantly. Yet even among the Koryak availability was limited, as the mushroom only grew in certain places. Supply was at its zenith at the beginning of winter, when as many mushrooms as could be found were gathered and dried. A moderate dose of two to four was normal, although ten to twelve were taken on special occasions or when supplies were plentiful. Among both the Koryak and Chukchee, the use of *Amanita muscaria* was not limited to shamans, but as a rule women did not consume it.

It was not only humans who were affected by this fungus. Georg Wilhelm Steller, a member of the Krasheninnikov Expedition to Eastern Siberia in the mid-eighteenth century, notes the following incident involving an intoxicated reindeer. The reindeer was seen staggering around in a stupor by some Koryak herders nearby; recognising the symptoms of fly-agaric intoxication, they tied up the beast and then slaughtered it. Its flesh – still containing the psychoactive properties of the fungus – was then distributed among those present who, soon afterwards, became intoxicated too. *Amanita muscaria* has the property, apparently unique among hallucinogenic species, of retaining its potency when voided in the form of urine. This property was known to many Siberians, who avidly drank their own or others' urine to achieve a state of intoxication, much to the disgust of many Russian and other observers of this curious custom. Although an early nineteenth-century account claims that the Koryak have known 'since time immemorial' that such urine is more potent than the fly-agaric itself, this is contradicted by the Russian anthropologist Waldemar Jochelson, who spent considerable time among the Koryak and mastered their language. Jochelson states that although the urine has an intoxicating effect it is, in fact, weaker than that of the fungus itself, as the Koryak themselves informed him.

The Koryak used a variety of methods of consumption. The most common was to roll the dried pieces of mushroom into a ball, which was then swallowed in a single gulp. Another was to cook the fungus in a soup, but more mushrooms were required to produce the same level of intoxication as when the mushroom pieces were simply swallowed. A third, more complicated, way was to soak it in a 'brandy' made from the juice of the bilberry (*Vacinium uliginosum*). The Koryak had learnt the art of distilling from the Cossacks and imitated it according to their means. The concoction was distilled in a large iron kettle with a wooden cover sealed with dough. An old gun-barrel served as a condenser. Koryak men are reported to have drunk their own urine after getting intoxicated on this brandy-mushroom cocktail, presumably to prolong its effects. Another infusion, in use among the Kamchadal, involved soaking fly-agaric and willow-herb together. The fungus was also boiled in water by some Russian settlers in Siberia, who drank the resulting brew as an alcohol substitute.

The effects of *Amanita muscaria* are diverse and vary according to dosage, method of preparation and the cultural and psychological expectations of the consumer. A small dose (or the initial effect of a larger one) causes bodily stimulation and a desire for movement and physical exercise. Under its influence a Koryak man is reported to have carried a 120 lb (some 55 kg) sack of flour a distance of ten miles, something he would not have been able to do normally. Such feats of physical strength and endurance have their mythic precedents. In one Koryak myth Big Raven (the Creator) asked

Existence for help to lift a heavy load. This deity told him to eat fly-agaric. He did so and was able to lift the load with ease. That the Creator himself is associated with the consumption of mushrooms again demonstrates the weakness of Eliade's view of the use of hallucinogens as a late and decadent aspect of Siberian spirituality.

Responses to the fly-agaric varied widely even among the Koryak. Sometimes an intoxicated individual had to be restrained from over-exerting himself, whilst on other occasions it would induce a tranquil state of bliss in which beautiful visions appeared before the eyes. The Russian anthropologist Waldemar Bogoras, who witnessed the Chukchee use of fly-agaric on many occasions at the turn of the century, notes that the effects can be divided into three basic stages, which sometimes overlap. About fifteen minutes after taking the mushrooms the stimulating effects begin and there is much loud singing and laughing. This stage is followed by auditory and visual hallucinations in conjunction with the sensation that things increase in size (in this state a tub of water is said to seem as deep as the sea). The visions are of fly-agaric men who sometimes have no neck or legs; their stout cylindrical bodies move around swiftly. The number of fly-agaric men seen depends on the number of mushrooms consumed. (This particular belief is reflected in the lore of the Yurak of Western Siberia, among whom a curious rationale for the usual dose of two and a half mushrooms is given.

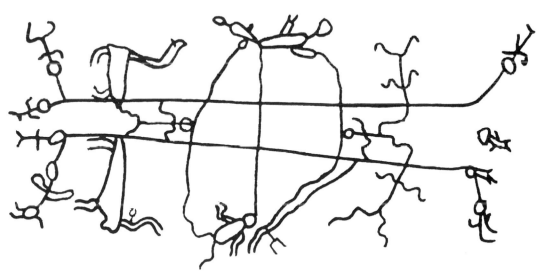

10 Chukchee sketch of the winding paths of the fly-agaric men seen during *Amanita muscaria* hallucinations. From Wasson 1971, fig. 10.

41

The two and a half fly-agaric men run ahead of the shaman in his visionary journey and the shaman is only able to keep up because the half-man runs more slowly, looking back as if waiting for the other half.) As the third stage begins, the user gradually loses awareness of his surroundings as the fly-agaric men grab him by the arms and take him along the intricate paths that lead to the other world. The routes taken by the fly-agaric men are shown in a Chukchee sketch brought back by Bogoras (fig. 10).

After the visions begin to fade, stupor, and then sleep, take over. The user awakes with all the symptoms of a hangover – a general feeling of weakness, a headache and often violent vomiting fits. A single mushroom starts the whole experience off again, and this 'hair of the dog' remedy is followed by seasoned users. Addicts, even when not under the influence, can easily be recognised by their haggard appearance, twitching faces and unsteady gait.

Jochelson gives a humorous account of his attempt to persuade a Koryak man to sing into the phonograph for the sake of posterity. The man, who was well known for his singing, was held back by shyness. By way of 'Dutch courage' he took two mushrooms and soon burst into song, gesticulating vigorously. Now, as Jochelson says, it was all he could do to restrain the man: 'I had to support him, lest he fall on the machine; and when the cylinder came to an end, I had to tear him away from the horn, where he remained bending over it for a long time, keeping up his songs.'[4]

Trade in fly-agaric among the Eastern Siberian tribes was a very profitable business. Russian attempts to outlaw such dealing were impossible to enforce, and among the Koryak a single piece of mushroom could be exchanged for a reindeer, while a whole one fetched three or four. By the beginning of the nineteenth century the Kamchadals, largely through their closer contacts with the Russians, gave up fly-agaric in favour of vodka. Yet they still continued to collect the mushroom and sell it to their Koryak neighbours. With the increased availability of alcohol and tobacco, fly-agaric use also declined among the Koryak and Chukchee, and the use of both these new intoxicants certainly signalled a change of direction from the old shamanic way. Yet this well-trodden path was not always as straight and narrow as Eliade would have us believe. Post-war reports of the use of mushrooms in the far north hint that there are probably still a few willing to follow the winding tracks of the fly-agaric men.[5]

Three
· · · · · · ·
The Mystery of *Haoma*

Indeed all other intoxications
are accompanied by Violence of the Bloody Club,
but the intoxication of *Haoma*
is accompanied by bliss-bringing Rightness.

Avesta: Yasna 10, 8

It is related from the Prophet that over each leaf and seed of the
isfand plant an angel is appointed so that through its bark and
roots and branches grief and sorcery are set aside.

Muhammad Baqir Majlisi, a Shi'a theologian

The Indo-Iranians (Aryans) were a pastoral people whose homeland was
somewhere in the Greater Iranian area (that is, north of India, west of China,
south of the boreal forests of Siberia and east of Mesopotamia). During the
second millennium BC they split into two separate groups. One branch, the
Indo-Aryans, went south and invaded the Indus Valley, whilst the other
remained in Central Asia. The earliest texts of these two peoples, the Indian
Rig Veda and the Iranian *Avesta*, although only written down much later,
preserve the most archaic forms of both language groups. Both texts mention
a plant (Indian *soma*, Iranian *haoma*) that was the focus of an important act
of worship (Indian *yajna*, Iranian *yasna*). The identity of this plant, however,
remains a mystery and has been the subject of vigorous debate.

The rituals described in the *Rig Veda* and the *Avesta* centred on the preparation, purification and consumption of the plant, which was originally
pounded in a stone mortar, strained through a sieve of bull's hair, mixed
with water and other ingredients, then consecrated to the gods before being
consumed. Although such rituals continue in modified form today, the
priests of both religious traditions have long since lost knowledge of the
original plant and use non-intoxicating substitutes in its place.

The Mystery of Haoma

The once popular idea that *soma* was an alcoholic beverage of some kind has been demonstrated to be erroneous. In the *Rig Veda* fermented drinks (*sura*) are clearly distinguished from *soma*, and this division is reiterated in the later Indian sources such as the *Brahmanas* (*c.* 800 BC). Practical objections have also been levelled at this suggestion: the stalks of the plant were pressed as part of the liturgical act and the resulting juice was consumed before the ritual was over, so clearly there was no time for the process of fermentation to take place. However, despite the strong arguments against any links with alcohol, this theory still occasionally recurs, and the German pharmacologist Hummel has suggested that *soma* was *Rheum palmatum* or some other species of rhubarb (none of which have psychoactive properties), crushed and fermented with honey or some other source of sugar.[1] Various scholars have put forward hashish as another candidate, but the Vedic descriptions of *soma* as a 'fragrant liquor' (*Rig Veda* IX, 113) and a drink 'crushed from the juice of the plant' (X, 85, 3) do not correspond at all with methods of cannabis preparation. Another popular idea is that *soma* may have been a type of leafless climbing plant, perhaps a species of *Periploca, Sarcostemma* or *Ephedra*.

An entirely different theory was proposed by the Wall Street banker and amateur mycologist R. Gordon Wasson. In the 1950s Wasson would meet friends for lunch to discuss, among other things, his burning passion for mushrooms – particularly hallucinogenic species. Among his fellow diners was Aldous Huxley, whose *Brave New World* (1932) features a drug called *soma*. Huxley had experimented with various hallucinogens and was well acquainted with Wasson's rediscovery of the use of psychoactive mushrooms in Mexico. It was during one of these lunches that Wasson suggested to Huxley and Stephen F. de Borhegyi (a specialist on the use of mushrooms in ancient Mesoamerica) that the intoxicant *soma* might be none other than the fly-agaric.

By 1968 Wasson had marshalled a vast and impressive array of materials to support his idea and published them in *Soma: Divine Mushroom of Immortality.* That *soma* might have been a mushroom had never previously been suggested, and Wasson's brilliant book revived the rather flagging interest in the identity of *soma* among the scholarly community and presented a strong challenge to all previous attempts to unravel the mystery. Wasson took the *Rig Veda* as his main source. In these texts *soma* is described in a number of ways – mainly in metaphor – and there are no direct botanical references (which is not surprising, since the Vedic priests could hardly be expected to share the interests of modern researchers). Wasson points out that nowhere in the entire *Rig Veda*, consisting of over a thousand hymns, is there any reference to the root, leaves, blossoms or seeds of the *soma*.[2] He thinks it unlikely that there was a conspiratorial silence by the priests to hide these obvious attributes of most chlorophyll-bearing plants, and that it is more probable that the *soma* plant had neither root nor leaves, blossoms nor seeds: a mushroom is thus the ideal candidate, as it lacks all these features common to most other plants. Furthermore, there is no mention of the cultivation of *soma*, and the fly-agaric is notoriously difficult to cultivate even under modern laboratory conditions. The Vedas also state that *soma* grew in the mountains and never speak of it growing elsewhere. Although the fly-agaric grows at sea-level in northern Eurasia, in the Indo-Iranian cultural region its growth is limited to the mountainsides of the Hindu Kush and the Himalayas at the considerable height of 8,000 to 16,000 feet (approx. 2,500–5,000 m). The fact that *soma* is only said to grow in the mountains is used by Wasson to strengthen the case for the elimination of other potential identifications:

> What a useless business it is for us to go chasing in the valleys after rhubarb, honey, hashish, wild Afghan grapes; in hot arid wastes after species of Ephedra, Sarcostemma, Periploca![3]

However, the Indo-Aryans only conquered the valleys and thus could not have had direct access to the fly-agaric growing in the mountain regions. To get round this awkward fact Wasson conjectures that they must have obtained supplies of the fungus by trading with hostile mountain tribes.

Wasson's theory leans heavily on his attempt to show that the unique property of fly-agaric as an intoxicant that remains psychoactive in the consumer's urine is attested in the texts of the *Rig Veda* and the *Avesta*. Two particular passages are stressed by the author. The first comes from the *Rig Veda* IX, 74:

> Soma, storm cloud imbued with life, is milked of ghee, milk. Navel of the Way, Immortal Principle, he sprang into life in the far distance. Acting in concert, those charged with the office, richly gifted, do full honor to Soma. The swollen men piss the flowing [*soma*].

The other, said to be the words of the ancient Iranian prophet Zarathustra (Zoroaster), is from *Yasna* 48, 10:

> 'When will thou do away with this urine of drunkenness with which the priests evilly delude [the people]?'

Wasson outlines the life history of *Amanita muscaria* in order to show the aptness of the descriptions in the Vedas. In autumn the fly-agaric appears at the foot of the birch and pine, first emerging as a little white ball like cotton wool. It swells rapidly and bursts its white garment, the fragments of the envelope remaining as patches on the brilliant red skin beneath; often, after it has rained, the cap is washed clean revealing the resplendent scarlet head in all its glory. When it is gathered it changes colour to a dull chestnut hue, and when it is crushed the extracted juice is tawny yellow. This range of colours is covered by the Vedic term *hari* which is frequently used to describe the appearance of *soma*. As there are no references to it being green, it seems improbable to Wasson that any of the chlorophyll-bearing plants are likely candidates for *soma*.

Wasson's interpretation of Vedic passages, which seem to indicate priestly knowledge of the life history of the mushroom, contradicts his admission that the Indo-Aryan valley dwellers did not have direct access to the plant, but were reliant on others for fresh supplies. If they did not have access to the mushroom *in situ*, how can they have known the details of its growth? Wasson's not very convincing response to such objections is to suggest that at least some of the priests must have known the fly-agaric in its natural state. Metaphors in the Vedas that 'fit like a glove' if applied to the fly-agaric include the likening of *soma* to an udder and a teat. The udder is, for Wasson, a reference to the protuberant cap of the mushroom which is milked for its juice, whilst the teat may suggest the stipe (or stalk) of the plant. *Soma* is also called the 'mainstay of the sky' and in Wasson's ingenious reading of the metaphor this is a reference to the robust stipe which holds up the hemispherical cap, itself reminiscent of the vault of the heavens.

Wasson also draws on the importance of the mushroom in Chinese and Siberian culture to strengthen his case. Such parallels are of secondary importance and, although they are fascinating topics in themselves, do not clinch the case for fly-agaric use among the Indo-Iranians. His overall theory has been accepted by a variety of scholars including the botanist Richard Evans Schultes, the anthropologists Claude Lévi-Strauss and Weston La Barre, and the poet and writer on classical subjects Robert Graves. Yet the Indologist John Brough has voiced the opinion, shared by some of his fellow Vedic specialists, that the answer to the mystery of *soma* cannot be adduced from the *Rig Veda*. He criticises Wasson for having decided *a priori* that *soma* was the fly-agaric and then distorting data from the Vedas to fit this preconception. Wasson, in a rejoinder to Brough, has criticised him in turn for living in an isolated 'hermetic coterie' and not seeking out possible solutions beyond the strict confines of the Vedas. However, whilst the specialists can be accused of resenting a solution discovered by an outsider, the lack of support from those who know the Vedas best cannot be lightly disregarded. Even Wendy Doniger (O'Flaherty), who compiled a history of the study of *soma* for Wasson's own book, has suggested that the search for an original *soma* plant is perhaps futile and that all later substitutes (including, possibly, fly-agaric) were surrogates for a mythical plant that never existed except in the minds of the early priests. Whilst such a view reiterates the pessimism of Vedists towards reaching a botanical identification of *soma* from their primary sources, it cannot be accepted as a solution. A substance of such cultural importance cannot be conjured away as purely imaginary, and it is difficult to see why something literally insubstantial should ever have been replaced by real plant substitutes.

More general criticisms have been levelled at Wasson's theory; of these, three are of particular significance. The weakness of his claim that the Vedic priests must have had to trade to obtain their supplies of *soma*/fly-agaric, yet were apparently able to describe the fleeting details of its growth far away in the mountains, has already been noted. Secondly, the descriptions of *haoma* in the *Avesta* do not suggest a mushroom, for in this Iranian source the plant in question is said to be tall, perfumed and greenish. The third point of contention concerns the apparent hints in the *Rig Veda* and the *Avesta* as to the drinking of psychoactive (human) urine, on which Wasson's thesis largely stands or falls. The Vedic reference to the urination of *soma* is not as clear-cut as Wasson would probably have liked. Even presuming that it is meant literally, it still does not refer to priests as such but simply to men; nor does it make any mention of the urine being drunk. Concerning the Avestan passage cited by Wasson, two recent translations and commentaries by Iranian linguists are instructive. Helmut Humbach's translation retains the basic meaning of the earlier one used by Wasson:

'When will (someone) kick over the (vessels of) urine of that (demon of) intoxication?'[4]

However, in his commentary Humbach notes that the yellow *haoma* drink in the vessels is likened to urine on account of its colour but not that it actually is urine. Martin Schwartz's reading is more radical: he suggests that the word translated as intoxication or drunkenness, *madahya*, is a probable scribal error for *magahya*, which has an entirely different meaning. Furthermore, he asserts that *muthrem* means 'filth' or 'excrement' and not, as

Wasson suggests, 'urine'. In Schwartz's view neither intoxication nor urine feature in the passage, thus weakening the case that it hints at the use of psychoactive urine derived from fly-agaric consumption.[5]

Although there are good reasons to doubt that either of these passages from the ancient period supports his theory, Wasson is able to cite examples of urine drinking in later Indian culture. There is an episode in the *Mahabharata* in which Krishna offers a disciple the urine of an outcast hunter to drink. This lowly hunter turns out to be Indra (who was the chief god of the Indo-Aryans) and the urine itself a draught of immortality. For Wasson, this incident is a survival of the earlier fly-agaric cult. Modern instances of urine drinking in India are also brought forward as corroborating evidence by Wasson, but David Stophlet Flattery notes that:

> The recycling of one's own urine for therapeutic purposes in modern India, to which Wasson draws attention, appears to reflect the influence of the popular book *Human Urine, An Elixir of Life*, by Rajivbhai Manibhai Patel (1963), the precedent for whose self experiments with urine drinking came not from Indian tradition but from 20th century Arkansas.[6]

The impression given by Flattery, namely that the custom is not known historically on the subcontinent, is misleading. In fact there are other references in Indian literature to urine as an elixir. In the classic yoga manual *Siva Samhita* it is said that the yogin can transmute base metals into gold by rubbing them with his own excrement or urine. The Aghori ascetics of contemporary Benares in Northern India, who practise many inversions of 'normal' religious activities (such as eating the flesh of corpses and consorting with prostitutes), describe urine in their ritual language as *amari pan*, which the anthropologist Jonathan Parry relates to the Hindi word *amrit* meaning 'nectar of immortality'.[7]

The Zoroastrians of both Iran and India have used cattle urine – but not human urine – in their religious life. Unconsecrated urine, used for outward cleansing, is known as *gomez* (or by the circumlocutory Dari term *pajow*). It is viewed as a proper form of disinfecting unclean things and is taken directly from any bull, cow or calf. *Nirang*, or consecrated bull's urine, is used for inward cleansing, that is to say it is drunk. Urine used for this purpose is ideally taken from a white bull calf, which is considered to be the purest animal. It is consecrated for seven successive nights by a special ritual called *Vendidad* and then stored in sealed glass jars for a further forty days in either a cellar or a hole in the ground, after which it is ready to be consumed at a ritually appropriate time. Ideally it should be stored as long as possible, seven years being considered auspicious, five of them underground and the last two above ground. A priest living in the Zoroastrian stronghold of Yazd in Iran was reliably reported to have kept *nirang* for forty years.

Although these examples from India and Iran show that the drinking of urine for its alleged therapeutic and spiritual effects is far from rare in traditional beliefs and practices, there is no reason to connect them with the fly-agaric mushroom. Such uses of urine are by no means restricted to the Indian and Iranian civilisations. By 1891 Captain John Bourke, an American cavalry officer and amateur ethnologist, had collected a variety of accounts of the use of urine from many different parts of the world. It has been utilised in industry (for tanning, bleaching and dyeing), for hair washing, as a medicine, as a ceremonial ablution and as an ingredient in the concoctions of witches and sorcerers. Alien as such practices may seem, Bourke cites cases from the 1880s in which urine was drunk for medical reasons in both Staffordshire (England) and New York.[8]

One of the sensations of fly-agaric intoxication is the perceiving of things or persons out of scale, either larger (macroscopia) or smaller (microscopia). This became widely known in the West through the work of Lewis Carroll (Charles Dodgson), who had read a review of Mordecai Cooke's work on British fungi, containing an account of *Amanita muscaria* and its macroscopic and microscopic properties. This notion was used to good effect in Carroll's popular *Adventures of Alice in Wonderland*. Macroscopia is mentioned in the records of Siberian mushroom use (see p. 41) and Indian sources also note such experiences – although without reference to fly-agaric. One of the early yogic texts, the *Hathayogaprapidaka*, contains a list of *siddhis* (or psychic powers) which includes *animan*, or the power to become as small as an atom, and *mahiman*, the power to become as large as space. In the *Yoga-sutras* Patanjali states that ecstasy-inducing drugs are a means of obtaining such psychic powers, and the use of drugs in Indian mystical contexts is well attested – opium, hashish and various *Datura* species among them. There is no reason to think that the macroscopia and microscopia discussed by the yogins had any connection with the fly-agaric, as such sensations can be produced by other means, with or without intoxicants.

Haoma and harmel

Wasson's identification of *soma/haoma* has thus been shown to be open to serious doubt on various fronts, and if the solution to the mystery cannot be found in the Vedas nor in Siberian, Chinese or later Indian parallels then the Iranian sources are the only viable option. Wasson's marginalisation of the *Avesta* in favour of the 'purer' traditions of the *Rig Veda* is questionable for, although the latter is earlier in date, this does not necessarily mean it reflects Indo-Iranian traditions more truly. The original *soma/haoma* must have grown in the Greater Iranian area, and the Iranian sources are more likely to preserve lore concerning the plant than those of the Indo-Aryans who left the homeland far behind.

Two theories put forward in recent years on the identity of *soma/haoma* concentrate on the Iranian sources. The first, by Gernot Windfuhr, identifies it as ginseng, partly on the grounds that both the *Avesta* and *Rig Veda* describe the plant as shaped like the human body (rather like the mandrake, see Chapter 6). However, although the ginseng root does resemble the human body and is used as an effective tonic in traditional Chinese medicine, its minimal psychoactive effects hardly make it a serious candidate for *soma/haoma*. Furthermore, ginseng does not grow in the area in question, as Windfuhr himself admits. His argument degenerates into an irrelevant discussion of Chinese and Iranian star lore that does little to help his case, and the apologetic conclusion that ginseng is 'at least a fairly good choice for *Haoma/Soma* considering that we may be running out of natural candidates'[9] hardly inspires confidence.

The other recent theory, put forward by Flattery and Schwartz, does not attempt to identify a new 'natural candidate' but takes as its starting point one of the earliest Western suggestions, made by Sir William Jones. In 1794 Jones published his translation of the Indian work *The Laws of Manu*, in which he describes *soma* as a species of mountain rue. Flattery notes that it was not a genuine species of rue (of the genus *Ruta*) that was meant, but rather harmel or wild rue (*Peganum harmala*, see fig. 11) which, in traditional Persian ethnobotany, is considered the wild variety of the genuine rue species that grows in Iran (*Ruta graveolens*). Harmel is a woody perennial shrub found in both the Central Asian steppes and the Iranian Plateau; therefore, unlike either fly-agaric or ginseng, it would have been available to many Indo-Iranian groups in their original homeland. Moreover, vestiges of its once prominent role in religious life are still found among the peoples of the region. In contemporary Iranian folk medicine the psychoactive

11 Harmel (*Peganum harmala*).

properties of harmel are recognised; to consume an infusion made from its seeds is believed to induce madness. In central Iran it is still boiled in vinegar to alleviate toothache; as the dilute acetic acid releases almost all the psychoactive alkaloids in the seeds, this remedy should not be swallowed. If this is done, either accidentally or deliberately, a soporific stupor results, accompanied by hallucinations. At Bukhara in Central Asia the inhalation of the smoke of burning harmel seeds was practised by 'village fools' to induce euphoria, yet as a rule the seeds are burned not for their intoxicating properties but for the snapping sounds and pungent fumes, which are said to ward off evil spirits. The seed is also widely used to produce the 'Turkish red' dye typical of many Persian and Turkish carpets.

Flattery's study of the descriptions of harmel (known in Persian as *isfand*) in texts from the Islamic period has shown remarkable parallels with the qualities attributed to *haoma* in the *Avesta* – too many parallels to be dismissed as mere coincidence. For example, in the *Avesta* it is said that Yima, Athwya, Thrita and Pourushaspa (Zarathustra's father) preceded Zarathustra in the cult of *haoma*, whilst the Islamic tradition attributes the use of *isfand* to Muhammad (or, in some instances, Ali), Fatima (the Prophet's daughter) and her sons Husayn and Hasan. In *Yasna* 9, 26 the Supreme Being, Ahura Mazdah, is said to have imbued *haoma* with spiritual efficacy,

51

whilst Muhammad is instructed by Allah to use *isfand*. *Yasna* 10,1 states that if *haoma* is kept in the house of righteous people it has the power to avert evil spirits, and the Islamic sources assign a similar prophylactic function to *isfand*. In *Yasna* 9 there are references to *haoma* giving its users courage, and a *hadith* (a saying attributed to the Prophet) relates that Muhammad, in seeking a solution to the cowardice of his followers, was told by Allah to command them to consume *isfand* in order to make them brave. It is not only in the *Avesta* that the chosen plant of ancient times is attributed with the power of giving courage: *soma* was said by the Vedic priests to have acted as a powerful stimulant to warriors, and this is epitomised by the bellicose god Indra who drank it. This attribute of *soma/haoma* is compatible with the qualities of *isfand* but not with the fly-agaric, for, as Wasson himself states, the mushroom does not cause warlike behaviour.[10]

The case for *haoma* being harmel is therefore strong both in terms of the latter's geographical distribution and in the historical continuity demonstrated by the parallels between the archaic period and Islamic times. It only remains to compare the psychoactive properties attributed to *haoma* with the known effects of the active alkaloids contained in harmel.

The visions of Wiraz and the vine

> For the soul's journey (haoma) is the best food.
>
> *Avesta: Yasna* 9,16

The most comprehensive account of the use of an intoxicant in Zoroastrian literature is to be found in the *Book of Arda Wiraz*, dating from the ninth century AD but originally composed at a much earlier time, perhaps before the third century AD. This text details the visions of the religious hero Arda Wiraz under the influence of *mang*, a psychoactive drug which there is good reason to identify with the original *haoma*. Wiraz drinks *mang* from three golden cups, following the *Yasna* rite, which traditionally involves the swallowing of *haoma* in three draughts. The story begins with a description of a great meeting of Zoroastrian priests and pious followers of the faith who, in the wake of the damage done to their religion by the invasion of Alexander the Great, decided to send the most righteous man among them to the spirit world to find out if the prayers and ceremonies they were performing were correct in the eyes of God. Before consuming the intoxicant which would transport him there, Wiraz washed his hands and body, put on fresh clothes, perfumed himself with scent and spread out a new carpet. His consumption

of the three cups of *mang* was accompanied by the invocations Good
Thought, Good Speech and Good Action, according to the tenets of the faith.
He remained in a trance for seven days and nights whilst the priests and the
faithful recited prayers over him and kept watch. During this time Wiraz's
soul travelled to the other world, returning to his body only on the seventh
day. When he awoke he asked for a meal in order to restore his strength and
afterwards related all that he had seen in his visions to a waiting scribe.

Wiraz was accompanied on his spiritual journey by two beneficent spirits,
who took him across the Chinvat Bridge that led to the other world. He was
taken to both heaven and hell, where he saw the rewards bestowed upon
the righteous and the punishments inflicted on evil-doers. Of heaven he
says: 'I . . . saw the pre-eminent world of the pious, which is the all-glorious
light of space, much perfumed with sweet basil, all-bedecked, all-admired,
and splendid, full of glory and every joy and every pleasure, with which no
one is satiated';[11] whilst among the visions of hell he saw 'the soul of a man
who, from head to foot, remained stretched upon a rack; and a thousand
demons trampled upon him, and ever smote him with great brutality and
violence. And I asked thus: "What sin was committed by this body?".' His
two spiritual guides, Srosh and Adar Yazad, inform him that it is 'the soul
of that wicked man who, in the world, collected much wealth; and he
consumed it not himself, and neither gave it, nor allowed a share, to the
good; but kept it in store'.[12]

That the visions of Wiraz were induced by harmel cannot be demonstrated
by direct comparisons with Islamic uses of the plant since, as I have already
said, the latter did not typically involve intoxication. The active alkaloids
contained in the harmel plant (harmine, harmaline and tetrahydroharmine)
are also found in various species of *Banisteriopsis (yajé)*, a jungle vine (liana)
utilised by Amazonian peoples to obtain visions (see Chapter 4). Since the
psychoactive substances are identical in both plants, Flattery has sought to
show that recurrent themes occur in both the Iranian and Amazonian visions,
thus strengthening his case that harmel is *haoma*.

Firstly, it is necessary to stress that there are considerable differences in
the visions experienced in the two traditions. These are due both to chemical
and cultural factors. Although harmel and *yajé* share the same alkaloids, the
preparation of both plants involves the use of secondary ingredients which
alter the structure and intensity of the experience of intoxication. Cultural
differences affect both the imagery perceived in the hallucinations and the
uses to which the altered state of consciousness is put. For example, visions
of jaguars are common in the Amazonian tradition, these animals being

intimately linked with shamanic themes (for a detailed account see pp. 66–7). Of course, such images are absent in the Iranian sources, as the jaguar is not found in Asia. Similarly, the use of *yajé* in the Amazon for the clairvoyant detection of criminal activities (such as the discovery of the identity of a thief, murderer or sorcerer) has no direct parallel in the Iranian use of harmel, although the purpose of Wiraz's visionary journey necessarily requires belief in some sort of clairvoyant faculty.

Despite these differences, the resemblance between the two traditions is striking. A common sensation in *yajé*-induced altered states of consciousness is that the soul separates from the physical body in order to travel to the spiritual world. This experience, often described as a flight of the soul, is usually achieved by the shamans, who are the spiritual specialists of their societies. Wiraz, too, is a spiritual adept, and the separation of his soul and body during his week-long trance presents a clear correspondence with the shamanic experiences from the Amazon. Also in both cases, the body of the visionary usually remains immobile during the trance, suggesting that this may be an effect partially caused by alkaloids common to both plants.

The spiritual world which the Amazonian Indians enter in their hallucinatory state is populated by both deities and demons, who are often perceived to be in combat. Such a dualistic view is also fundamental to ancient Iranian religion: the Zoroastrian teaching that there is a perpetual struggle between the forces of light and darkness is exemplified in Wiraz's descriptions of the fate of those souls who have chosen good or evil and are seen by him in their after-life stations in heaven and hell. One feature of the Zoroastrian world view which is often commented upon by historians of religion is that, in contrast to many other archaic belief systems, the spiritual beings described in the religious texts are not personifications of natural forces but embodiments of abstract moral principles. The cosmologies of certain Amazonian societies, such as the Tukano, are also highly abstract and are certainly related to *yajé* visions. Geometric motifs (i.e. entoptic phenomena or phosphenes) permeate Tukano culture; the images, seen in their visions, embody important social principles. The anthropologist Reichel-Dolmatoff has clearly demonstrated that the Tukano do not consider these geometric motifs to be based on natural objects but rather the opposite, that the phosphenes influence the structure of both nature and culture. If any use of geometric motifs in the Iranian tradition can be linked to the harmel plant, it is most likely to be in the realm of carpet designs. Is it perhaps possible that in earlier times harmel seeds were used not only for dyeing carpets, but that the geometric shapes commonly used in the designs were inspired by harmel intoxication? Furthermore, as Wiraz's spiritual flight took place whilst his body lay on a carpet, could it be that the legends of flying carpets are also to be explained by intoxication (just as the witches' flights on the broomstick are shown to be related to hallucinations: see Chapter 6)? Such speculations on the links between intoxication and carpets are, of course, difficult to prove, although such a line of research is worthy of further investigation.

Of all the suggested identifications of the mysterious *soma/haoma* plant, harmel is therefore the most convincing. Its widespread growth throughout the Indo-Iranian homeland provides the necessary geographical correspondence with *soma/haoma*, and its role in Iranian folklore and ethnobotany establishes a stronger case for cultural continuity than any of the other candidates. Harmel's psychoactive properties could clearly have caused many of the effects which the ancient texts attribute to *soma/haoma*; whilst the parallels with *yajé* strengthen the case for a pharmacological correspondence. By a mysterious coincidence – and it *can* only be a coincidence – among the Guarani Indians of the Amazon *Banisteriopsis* is known as *jauma*, which is pronounced 'haoma'.

Four
. . . .
American Dreams

Richard Evans Schultes, an expert on psychoactive flora, reports that, to date, around 100 species of hallucinogens have been discovered in the New World. This is a considerably larger number than the total of such plants growing in the Old World. Species of *Banisteriopsis*, already mentioned in previous chapters, play an important role in Amazonian shamanism and have received much attention from ethnobotanists and anthropologists

12 A vision induced by *yajé*: the artist enters a house ablaze with colour. Felt-pen drawing by Maximiliano, a Tukano Indian from the Colombian Amazon region. Collection of Stephen Hugh-Jones.

alike. The inhaling of hallucinogenic snuff mixtures – still practised in the Amazon today – was once a widespread cultural trait throughout northern South America, as the abundance of snuff trays and related artefacts in the archaeological record shows, and the use of psychoactive substances such as mushrooms in ancient and modern Mexico and of the peyote cactus in some North American Indian communities was integral to their religious life. The antiquity of the shamanic use of all these plants shows how the spiritual life of aboriginal Americans is permeated with visions drawn from hallucinatory experiences. Tobacco is also important in the religious heritage of the New World, and its role in peacemaking between Indian groups is well known.

Geometry and the jaguar

The Amazonian rainforests are rich in hallucinogenic plants and the indigenous inhabitants of the region have used them for untold centuries. Serious Western research into the nature of such plants began with the expeditions of Richard Spruce, an ethnobotanist who explored the Amazon and the Andes between 1849 and 1864. Among the psychoactive species he discovered was a jungle vine which he named *Banisteria caapi*; it has subsequently been renamed *Banisteriopsis caapi* (fig. 13). In addition to the complexities involved in botanical identification (a subject to which I shall shortly return), researchers have found it difficult to determine precisely the effects produced by particular hallucinogens, as they are often taken in conjunction with other intoxicants. For example, Emboden, in discussing Spruce's own experiences with the vine in question, writes:

> The character of Spruce was that of an abstemious man, and it was with no great pleasure that he was obliged to 'dispatch' a cup of the 'nauseous beverage' himself followed by a gourd full of Manihot root beer, which he took with 'secret loathing'. Were that not enough, he was then given a cigar two feet long and as full as his wrist, followed by a cup of palm wine. He retired to a hammock with a cup of coffee and 'the strong inclination' to vomit.[1]

Schultes, probably the leading authority on the botany of Amazonian hallucinogens, has drawn together some of the reasons for the confusion surrounding the plants in question, and the problems of *Banisteriopsis* identification in particular. *Banisteriopsis* preparations are known by a variety of local names – *yajé, pinde, ayahuasca, cadána, caapi* and *natena* among them –

13 *Banisteriopsis caapi.*
From Schultes in Furst
(ed.) 1972, fig. 9.

BANISTERIOPSIS *Caapi*

(Spruce ex Griseb.) Morton

and earlier investigators did not realise that all these were of the same genus of plants. For example, *yajé* had been (falsely) identified with two other vines, *Prestonia amazonica* and *Mascagnia psilophylla*, as well as with species of *Datura*. The local names also refer to concoctions based on *Banisteriopsis caapi* and its close relatives (including *Banisteriopsis inebrians*) but almost invariably with various secondary ingredients. These additions to the basic recipe vary from region to region and are often as yet unidentified. Moreover, some formulae are unique to one group of Indians, or even to a single shaman. Another factor compounding the difficulties of producing a general account of *yajé* potions is the diversity in methods of preparation. The most

58

commonly recorded processes involve either infusing *Banisteriopsis* bark in cold water or boiling the bark or the stems for long periods. Chewing the fresh bark and preparing it in the form of a snuff have also been reported.

Analysts of the chemical constituents of *yajé* have added to the confusion caused by some ethnobotanists and anthropologists. Apparently distinct active alkaloids, isolated from specimens of *Banisteriopsis*, were named tele-pathine (a reference to the supposed telepathic powers that *yajé* is said to produce), banisterine and yajeine. It has since been demonstrated that all three describe a single alkaloid named harmine.

Not wishing to compound the botanical and chemical confusion sur-rounding *yajé* with a variety of anthropological accounts of its diverse cul-tural uses, I have chosen instead to give a detailed account of a single ethnographic case, that of the Tukano Indians of the Colombian north-west Amazon. This is preferable on two counts. Firstly, the use of *yajé* among these particular people has been the focus of studies conducted over a number of years by the Colombian anthropologist Gerardo Reichel-Dolmatoff. Secondly, his meticulous writings on the structure and contents of *yajé*-induced altered states of consciousness have already been alluded to in the present work, both in relation to the possible analogies with Upper Palaeolithic art (see Chapter 1) and with reference to Flattery and Schwartz's identification of *haoma* with *Peganum harmala* (see Chapter 3).

The Tukano use *yajé* (although they themselves call it *caapi*, I shall retain the more common term) in a variety of contexts, both collectively and individually. Important among these are initiation ceremonies, funerals, quests by shamans for visions, and the diagnosis of ailments. Consumption is restricted to adult males, although both women and uninitiated boys may be present on occasions when it is used. Several pieces of the fresh vine are cut and then mashed to a pulp in a wooden trough. Cold water is then added. The mixture is strained and transferred to a special decorated ceramic vessel of the type shown in fig. 14. This pot is used exclusively for the *yajé* drink and should ideally be made by an old woman. The production process is invested with sexual symbolism (as are many other aspects of *yajé* consumption). The vessel is perceived as a uterus and, by extension, serves as a model of transformation and gestation. In the process of making it the old woman polishes it, inside and out, with a hard yellow stone. This stone is seen as 'a phallus which shapes'. The pot is ritually purified with tobacco smoke before the *yajé* is poured into it. It is then taken into the communal house where the ceremony is to take place. Participants in *yajé* ceremonies are often required to observe restrictions on their behaviour prior to the

14 Painted ritual vessel of the Barasana Indians, used in *yajé* ceremonies. The U-shape on the foot of the vessel is the 'door', or the 'vagina' through which the participants enter the body of the vessel in order to be reborn. From Reichel-Dolmatoff 1987, pl. xvia.

event. Such restrictions include following a prescribed diet and a period of sexual abstinence. Reichel-Dolmatoff describes the beginnings of a ceremony he witnessed:

> The men, adorned [with feathers] and painted, seat themselves on their stools, their backs turned to the entrance. When night falls, they light a large torch of pitch, located approximately in the center of the room. This torch gives off an intense red light. Now there begins a long ceremonial dialogue between the representatives of the

household and those of the exogamous phratry [i.e. members of an internal division of the tribe who marry outside their immediate group] invited to the event. The Creation Myth and the genealogies of the phratries are recited. The origins of humanity are commemorated with the phallic staff, which, equipped with a small sound chamber, serves as a rattle. Shortly thereafter, various musical instruments are played, such as flutes and whistles. The dances that follow are performed to the accompaniment of songs and the beating of large wooden tubes whose lower sections the men pound against the floor. In addition, the men wear seed rattles on their ankles and elbows. One musical instrument consists of a turtle shell with a piece of wax attached; the shell is held under the left arm while the wax is rubbed rapidly by the right hand, producing a sound like the croaking of a frog.[2]

An event which takes place in some versions of the Tukano Creation Myth is of particular interest. It involves a mythical being named *Yajé* Woman, who gave birth to the *yajé* plant in the form of a child. The men who were present at this event seized the child and tore it limb from limb. These men represent the ancestors of the various modern Tukano phratries and this mythical episode can be seen as a cultural explanation for the diversity of present-day forms of hallucinations. Nowadays each phratry consumes its own special *yajé* and these types produce distinctive visions which are easily identified by Tukano people. Although there are overlaps in the hallucinations seen by the various Tukano groups, each individual can recognise in his visions which elements belong to his own phratry and which to others. The shamans, who have specialist knowledge of *yajé*, are able, up to a point, to manipulate its effects. This is done by careful preparation of the brew and supervising the quantities of *yajé* consumed. Yet despite their considerable expertise there is no guarantee of a 'good trip'. *Yajé* visions often cause terror in the consumer, whilst many users are overcome by nausea. More positive hallucinations are usually of a sexual nature and, for a fortunate few, such visions are transmuted into a mystical union with the mythical age. This, the highest attainment in Tukano *yajé* experience, has been described by one of the Indians as 'spiritual coitus', a return to the cosmic uterus.

Although the structure of *yajé*-induced altered states of consciousness does not directly conform to Lewis-Williams' and Dowson's three-stage model (see Chapter 1), the same shift – from an initial period in which entoptic phenomena (i.e. phosphenes) are perceived alone, to one in which figurative images enter the field of vision – is found in Tukano experiences. The perception of phosphenes (circles, clusters of triangles, spirals, etc.) is based on the workings of the human neurological system and as such is not unique to the Tukano or any other one group. The figurative phase that follows these geometric visions involves the perception of culturally conditioned images (such as jaguars, snakes and mythical scenes). What is significant about the geometric images is that the Tukano use them to convey key concepts and values in their cultural code. Whilst staying among the Tukano, Reichel-Dolmatoff asked a number of men to draw their *yajé* visions. Noticing that the same signs occurred again and again in their drawings, he reproduced them separately on special cards. He then took these cards to the men and asked them what the individual signs meant. In most cases the interpretations given to the anthropologist were remarkably similar, indicating that each had a distinct and well-understood cultural meaning. Such is the importance of *yajé* in Tukano culture that paintings, architectural designs, pottery, furniture and musical instruments are all decorated with geometric motifs originally seen in hallucinations (see fig. 15). The Tukano also ascribe the origin of their music and dances to auditory hallucinations and visions induced by *yajé*. The altered states of consciousness produced by the vine are considered by them to be superior to mundane consciousness, and this is reflected in both their artistic decoration and in their investing of the motifs with important social meanings. How long *yajé* has played such a central role in Amazonian life is unclear, but similar motifs are found depicted in indigenous rock carvings of uncertain age and these resemblances hint at the probable antiquity of the use of such hallucinogens in Amerindian societies.

Among the plants most commonly employed in the making of narcotic snuffs are species belonging to the *Anadenanthera* genus, especially *A. peregrina*. The seeds of this tree are crushed into a powder to create a strong hallucinogen. The earliest account of the use of this snuff (under the name of *cohoba*) dates from the 1490s when Friar Ramón Pané of the Order of St Jerome, who had been instructed by Columbus to collect details of native ceremonies in the West Indies, recorded instances of this particular practice that he had personally witnessed. On Hispaniola the powder was snuffed into the nose by a foot-long cane. The effects were almost instantaneous; the snuffer became stupefied and, on regaining consciousness, perceived the world upside down, with people walking with their heads downward. The intoxicated individuals would speak aloud to the spirits, who were imperceptible to onlookers. It is generally assumed that the inhabitants of

Male organ The name of this sign in Tukano language is the same as that given to the fruit of the rubber tree, the latex of which is a milky-coloured liquid connected by the Tukano with semen.

Drops of semen Rows of circles or dots symbolising semen also represent a line of social descent, or by extension the continuity of life.

Thought Undulating vertical lines symbolise creative thought or the energy of the solar creator.

Incest The spiral symbolises incest and forbidden women. Because of its form it may also represent the snail and the whirlpool (a natural danger mirroring the social danger of incest).

15 Geometric forms seen in Tukano hallucinations, and their cultural meanings. After Reichel-Dolmatoff in Furst (ed.) 1972.

this region migrated from the South American mainland and it is likely that they brought the snuffing practice with them, as it is only in South America that *Anadenanthera peregrina* grows in a truly wild state. The centre of both the past and present usage of this type of snuff is the Orinoco Basin, where it is known as *yopo*. In some communities the consumption of *yopo* is restricted to shamans, whilst in others it is in general use among adult males for both hedonistic and religious purposes.

An eighteenth-century account of snuff-taking among the Otomac Indians of the same region states that the shells of large snails, burnt into the form of quicklime, were added to the powder to increase its psychoactive effects. The resulting snuff was said to be so potent that even the most seasoned users had only to put a finger that had been dipped in it near to their nose to go into a convulsion of sneezing. An interesting aspect of this account is the significant differences recorded in the effects of the snuff on the warlike Otomac and on their more passive neighbours. The former would whip themselves up into a battle frenzy, whilst the latter remained benign and peaceful throughout their intoxication. This clearly emphasises the importance of cultural factors in shaping the nature and orientation of altered states of consciousness.

Another intoxicating snuff, which was only discovered by Westerners at the beginning of this century, is prepared from the tree bark of species of the *Virola* genus, known in the north-west Amazon by a variety of names including *epená, ebene, paricá, yákee* and *yató*. Like the *Anadenanthera* mixtures it is, as a rule, used in ritual contexts, although purely hedonistic consumption has been reported. One method of preparing this snuff involves removing the soft inner layer of bark, drying it by gentle roasting over a fire, crushing the shavings of the bark and finally grinding them into a fine powder. This pungent brown snuff is usually administered in one of two main ways. In the first method a large dose of the powder is blown into the nostrils through a bamboo, reed or bird-bone tube. The second, illustrated in fig. 16, involves inhaling the mixture through Y-shaped snuffing tubes inserted into both nostrils. The stimulating effects of the *Virola* snuff are felt almost immediately and are announced by the dancing, singing, shouting and occasional fighting of the snuffers. This initial stage of intoxication dissipates with the onset of nausea and a loss of muscular co-ordination. A long period of stupor ensues in which auditory and visual hallucinations are experienced, including macroscopia and sensations of flying and levitating. In order to increase the potency of this snuff secondary ingredients are sometimes added. Among the known admixtures are the ashes of *Theobroma*

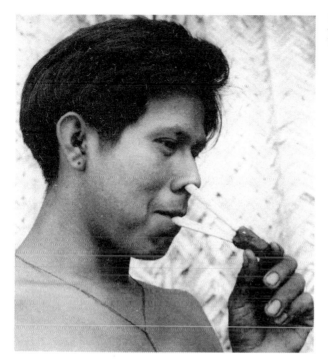

16 A Tukano Indian inhaling *virola* snuff. From Reichel-Dolmatoff 1987, pl. xviia.

subinacum (the cacao tree) and *Elizabetha princeps*. The leaves of the latter tree are said by the Waika Indians of Brazil to be 'the leaves of the Angel of Death'. This is no mere fanciful epithet: shamans are known to have died after snuffing this particularly powerful mixture.

Undoubtedly the commonest and most widely used snuffing material in the New World is tobacco. In South America today *Nicotiana tabacum* is used for this purpose, whilst *Nicotiana rustica* was favoured in ancient Mexico. The practice of snuffing probably originated in the Amazon Basin, but the use of a special tray for depositing the powder for its inhalation – a widespread cultural trait – may have been first developed on the Peruvian coast, where the oldest examples of such artefacts have been discovered. Several whalebone snuff trays found at the site of Huaca Prieta in Chicama Valley have been dated to about 1200 BC, as have four similar trays from the site of Asia in the Oma River Basin. In addition to these Peruvian examples, trays have been discovered at a number of archaeological sites in Colombia, Chile, Brazil, Argentina and elsewhere in northern South America. In most cases it is not clear what type of snuff was used. The snuff trays (sometimes called tablets) are made of a variety of materials including gold, although wood and stone are the most common. They are quite small, usually 10–30 cm (4–12 in) in length, and characterised by a shallow rectangular cavity that often has appendages or extensions carved with human or animal motifs. Such motifs are also found on the snuffing tubes and spatulas that accompany many of the pre-Hispanic trays. When these objects were first unearthed it was not clear to the early researchers what they were. It was suggested that the trays were used to hold blood offerings, or that they were palettes for mixing colours. That they are actually snuffing trays is demonstrated by ethnographic parallels from the Amazon Basin: both the shape of the cavity and the similarity of iconography confirm this identification.

The basic paraphernalia of snuffing consists of trays, tubes, spatulas, mortars and pestles, and snuff powder containers. The iconography of the designs on the trays is more complex and profuse than that of the other items. Constantino Manuel Torres has made a special study of six distinct regional iconographies of snuff trays from a variety of archaeological and ethnographic contexts in South America. Some of the motifs that make up these iconographies are clearly culture-specific. An instance of this is found on the only known example of a Tukano snuff tray, in the collection of the Oslo University Ethnographical Museum.[3] This tray is incised with a geometric motif familiar to the Tukano from their *yajé* visions. As I have already shown, although the perception of geometric images is a widely attested phenomenon, the meanings given to such signs by the Tukano are specific to their culture. The motif in question represents the gourd rattles of the Tukano and also the songs and spells that accompany their use. Geometric images do not as a rule feature prominently in the iconography of the snuff trays, but certain figurative motifs recur and are clearly of inter-cultural significance. Torres has demonstrated that three of these motifs are especially prevalent in both archaeological and ethnographic examples.

Felines, particularly jaguars, are depicted in a variety of ways on the snuff trays. Sometimes they occur in a purely zoomorphic form (see fig. 17) but more often in conjunction with human features. A human wearing a feline mask is common, particularly in examples from the archaeological sites of northern Chile. The meaning of such composite figures can be ascertained from the role of the jaguar in modern South American shamanism. Among the Tukano the same word is used for both jaguar and shaman, and their myths indicate that the central purpose of taking snuff is to transform the user into a jaguar. Felines are also commonly perceived in visions induced by a number of other hallucinogens, including *yajé*. The close relationship between jaguar and shaman may also be reflected in other snuffing equip-

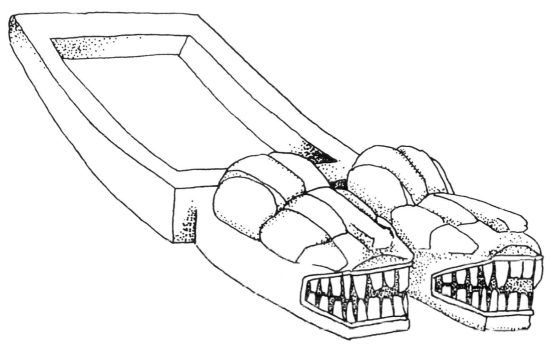

17 Wooden snuff tray from Lasana, Chile, with two feline heads. From Torres 1987, pl. 69 (original in Museo Arqueológico de Calama, Chile).

ment: Spruce, whilst travelling in the Orinoco Basin in the 1850s, noted a snuff container made from a jaguar's leg bone. That felines are frequently depicted on pre-Hispanic trays demonstrates the antiquity and tenacity of both shamanic lore in general and the particular role of hallucinogens in attaining spiritual knowledge.

The bird, as the most apt natural symbol for the ecstatic flight of the shaman, often features in hallucinogenic experiences and, not surprisingly, is an important motif in the iconography of the snuff trays. Bird-bone snuffing tubes were found alongside the earliest known trays (from Huaca Prieta), and similar items have been found in recent ethnographic contexts; in the River Tapajos region of Brazil snuffing tubes made from heron quills have been reported. Since birds feature prominently in the archaeological record, both in iconographic representations and in artefacts made from bone, their importance in modern shamanic visions is another clear example of the continuity of archaic American Indian traditions.

The third important animal motif found on both archaeological and ethnographic examples is the snake. Among the snuff trays of the Maué people of the Amazon this reptile is the most frequently depicted animal; this is probably related to the myth whereby the Maué had their origin in the union of a snake with a woman. This connection is strengthened by the sometimes distinctly phallic appearance of the snakes depicted. Other representations combining the snake image with features of jaguars and humans demonstrate that these key animal motifs are part of an interlocking nexus of shamanic lore. The jaguar, bird and snake share the ability to move easily between different natural domains. The agility of the jaguar on land is augmented in myth by an ability to move easily through water and air. The ability of birds to fly as well as to live on land, and the serpent's easy movement between land and water, make these creatures powerful prototypes for shamanic transformations. The dramatic changes in consciousness that occur during hallucinatory experiences require the shaman to be master of the elements of the inner world, just as these creatures are masters of the natural world.

'Magic mushrooms', amphibians and water-lilies

The Americas were first populated by Asiatic hunters who crossed the Bering Strait land bridge (known to scientists as Beringia) from north-east Asia. This exodus from Siberia took place at least 12,000 years ago: the numerous attempts to establish earlier dates for the migration into the New World have not – at least so far – received general acceptance. La Barre has suggested that the shamanic culture of the incoming people may have predisposed them actively to seek out ecstatic experiences induced by psychoactive plants. The data on the use of hallucinogenic fungi in North America is rather scanty compared with the wealth of documentation on such practices in Siberia and in Mexico. Yet this lack of evidence may not reflect indigenous attitudes to fungi so much as those of the investigators themselves, the majority of whom have been Anglo-Saxons. According to Lévi-Strauss, the Anglo-Saxons are notorious mycophobes whose revulsion for, and ignorance of, the various types of fungi has much to do with the poverty of information on their use in North American societies. Lévi-Strauss (himself a mycophile, or mushroom lover) has gathered together the disparate references to fungi in native American societies and lists a wide range of their cultural uses – as raw and cooked food, as a source of pigment used in painting, as a medicinal plaster and even as a sort of soap. He notes that of all Indian groups the Coast and Interior Salish are the most obviously mycophiles.

Captain John Bourke relates a story told to him in 1886 by a Mr Kennard of the United States Coast Survey. According to Kennard, the Indians of the Cape Flattery area (although he does not give any indication of which Indian group he is referring to, it seems likely to be the Coast Salish, as Cape Flattery is within their traditional homeland) drank a 'vile liquor' made by their medicine men out of potatoes and other (unspecified) ingredients. The drinker of such a brew was said to urinate immediately after consuming it. He then offered his urine for another to drink. Both the brew itself and the urine of the partakers were said to cause temporary insanity, delirium and eventual stupor. Since the fly-agaric is the only known hallucinogen that remains potent in the urine it seems safe to assume that the Coast Salish used *Amanita muscaria* in their ceremonial life. The Dogrib Athapaskans of the MacKenzie mountains in the Western Sub-Arctic are also known to use the fly-agaric in shamanistic rituals, and Lévi-Strauss notes that certain Eskimo (i.e. Inuit) and Athapaskan groups chew the ashes of a fungus that grows on birch trees (the main host of the fly-agaric), sometimes in conjunction with tobacco, which is said to increase its potency.

The Ojibway Indians of the Lake Superior area in Michigan used the fly-agaric in their annual ceremonies. In their language, which belongs to the Algonquian group, it is known as *Oshtimisk Wajashkwedo*, or 'red-top mushroom'. The Reverend Charles Lallemand wrote in 1626 that the Algonquian people of the region of Quebec believed in the immortality of the soul and that after death they would go to heaven, where their souls would eat mushrooms and communicate with each other. The Algonquins' knowledge of potent fungi is suggested in Longfellow's poem *Hiawatha*:

> Paused to rest beneath a pine tree,
> From whose branches trail the mosses,
> And whose trunk was coated over
> With the Dead Man's Moccasin Leather,
> With the fungus white and yellow.
>
> (Canto ix)

The ancient art of the Mayan people of Southern Mesoamerica included among its motifs depictions of mushrooms, frogs or toads, and water-lilies. Marlene Dobkin de Rios has suggested that all three were incorporated into

18 Two Highland Maya mushroom stones: (*left*) a jaguar, and (*right*) a frog or toad. 1500–500 BC. After V. P. Wasson and R. G. Wasson. 'The Hallucinogenic Mushrooms', *Garden Journal*, January/February 1958.

the art on account of their psychoactive properties, which, she believes, were utilised by shamans and priests. Over a hundred mushroom-shaped stones and associated ceramics have been discovered in Mesoamerica (fig. 18). These stones, found mainly in Highland Guatemala, were interpreted in the nineteenth century as phallic symbols and it was only subsequently that their true nature was realised. A tomb has been discovered which contains several small mortars that may have been used to crush mushrooms or *ololiuqui* seeds (another hallucinogen). The mortars are decorated with the frog/toad motif. This motif and that of the water-lily also occur on ceramics and sculptures and in the form of illustrations in Mayan texts. The thesis of Dobkin de Rios has been given a mixed critical reception and I shall consider the motifs separately for the sake of clarity.

To support her case Dobkin de Rios cites De Borhegyi's specialist studies of the mushroom stones and associated pottery. De Borhegyi suggests that these objects were used in sacred ceremonies which involved the ritual consumption of hallucinogenic mushrooms. Emboden, in commenting upon a particular mushroom stone found in Guatemala notes that the depiction of a young woman using a metate (the word derives from the Aztec *metatl* and refers to a flat or somewhat hollowed stone upon which grain, cocoa, etc. is ground by means of a smaller stone), suggests that they were used to crush mushrooms for consumption. The widespread use of psychoactive substances in Amerindian cultures has been seen by some writers (including Furst) to strengthen the case for their use in Mayan culture. Proskouriakoff, whilst accepting the likelihood of their use in Highland Guatemala, does not feel that the role of hallucinogens in Classic lowland Mayan civilisation can be demonstrated on these grounds alone. She dismisses the argument as a flight of fancy, noting that Dobkin de Rios herself admits there is no documentary or archaeological evidence to prove this particular assertion.

Dobkin de Rios also accepts that although the Maya might have used a species of toad (*Bufo marinus*) for its supposed hallucinogenic qualities, this is equally difficult to prove. Many of the known instances of this motif do not allow the observer to distinguish clearly whether it is in fact a frog or a toad. To pinpoint these images as representing a particular species is, in most cases, impossible. A further reservation to her thesis is that the frog/toad motif has other well-established symbolic functions in Mayan art. Its associations with rain and agriculture are widely accepted. Nicholas Hellmuth highlights the hypothetical nature of connecting the motifs with intoxication when, noting that indigenous women in the Central Market of Guatemala City sell various types of frog-shaped ceramics, he asks:

> Do these little old ladies secretly imbibe mind-expanding doses of toad-juice cocktail under their counters? Does the portrayal of mushrooms and toads in ancient art prove the ingestion of these substances by the ancient Maya?[4]

The species in question, *Bufo marinus* (the giant toad, fig. 19), is native to Central and South America. It is now also found in the West Indies, Florida, Hawaii, Australia and the Philippines, where it was introduced to control agricultural pests. *Bufo marinus* has poison glands located behind its eyes. A Mayan glyph dating from the seventh century AD depicts a toad with three circles at the back of its head which represent the poison glands. This seems to indicate knowledge of the toad as a source of poison, but not necessarily as a hallucinogen. Two particular poisons are found in the secretions of *Bufo*, bufotenine and buftalin. These are dangerous to the heart and only low doses or special techniques of preparation can limit their extreme toxicity. Traditional knowledge of such precautions continues to this day. Timothy Knab has taped an interview with a *curandero* (folk healer)

19 The giant toad (*Bufo marinus*).

from Veracruz in Mexico in which the precise method of extracting *Bufo* venom and reducing its toxic effects is given. Both frog and toad toxins are included by South American Indians in the preparation of poisonous arrows used in hunting. The deadly effects of such arrows are attributed by the German toxicologist Gustav Schenk not to the toad poisons themselves but to other ingredients (ptomaines). The Amahuaca of Peru are reported to use frog or toad poison by applying it into self-inflicted skin burns. This causes a state of trance in which the hunters believe themselves to be in contact with the spirits of animals and the forest.

Bufotenine is also present in *Amanita muscaria* (recently found to be growing in Highland Guatemala) and in the intoxicating *cohoba* snuff used in the Orinoco Basin. Whether it is an active ingredient in this snuff is still a matter of some dispute. Yet there are references to the potency of *Bufo* extracts. The seventeenth-century English friar Thomas Gage states that the Pokomam, a Highland Maya group, put poisonous toads in their fermented beverages in order to increase their intoxicating powers. The unusual discovery of a large number of *Bufo marinus* remains at the oldest known Olmec site, San Lorenzo in Veracruz (1200–900 BC), may point to a similar usage in earlier times. Given the disagreement over the properties of bufotenine and the lack of direct evidence for the use of *Bufo marinus* in the Classic Maya culture, Dobkin de Rios' suggestion remains just that. But it is an exciting suggestion and one which may yet be shown to be correct. The role of the toad in providing psychoactive ingredients for European witches' brews is equally contentious (see Chapter 6).

The New World water-lily (*Nymphaea ampla*), the third of the Maya motifs considered by Dobkin de Rios, has been demonstrated by Dr José Diaz to contain apomorphine-like compounds. Emboden's researches into another species of water-lily (*Nymphaea caerulea*) show that it is used by certain North African groups as a hypnotic and an effective substitute for opium. It also features in ancient Egyptian iconography, often in conjunction with the opium poppy and the mandrake. The Asian lotus plant, which also belongs to the family Nymphaeaceae, contains opiate-like alkaloids. These findings, hinting at the possible role of such plants in ancient religious life, are suggestive, but proof that the Maya used the water-lily as an intoxicant is still lacking.

No such doubts exist where the use of mushrooms by the Aztecs is concerned. They used hallucinogenic species which they named *teonanacatl*, meaning 'flesh of the gods'. Fray Bernardino de Sahagún, a sixteenth-century Franciscan missionary and author of the *General History of the Things of New Spain* (the *Florentine Codex*), describes their consumption and the subsequent effects:

At a banquet the first thing the Indians ate, was a black mushroom which they call nanácatl. These mushrooms caused them to become intoxicated, to see visions and also to be provoked to lust. They ate the mushrooms before dawn when they also drank cacao. They ate the mushrooms with honey and when they began to feel excited due to the effect of the mushrooms, the Indians started dancing, while some were singing and others weeping. Thus was the intoxication produced by the mushrooms. Some Indians who did not care to sing, sat down in their rooms, remaining there as if to think. Others, however, saw in a vision that they died and thus cried; others saw themselves being eaten by a wild beast; others imagined that they were capturing prisoners of war; others that they were rich or that they possessed many slaves; others that they committed adultery and had their heads crushed for this offence; others that they had stolen, some articles for which they had to be killed, and many other visions. When this mushroom intoxication had passed, the Indians talked over amongst themselves the visions they had seen.[5]

The use of hallucinogenic mushrooms has continued in Mexico up to the present day, especially in the area of Oaxaca. In 1936 Roberto J. Weitlaner became the first Westerner to witness sacred *teonanacatl* rites in the region. He was followed just before the Second World War by the young Richard Schultes, who collected various hallucinogenic species including *Stropharia (Psilocybe) cubensis*, a very potent variety. Emboden calculates that three or four dried *Stropharia* mushrooms have an equivalent effect to about thirty dried *Psilocybe mexicana*. R. G. Wasson made a number of trips to Oaxaca, beginning in 1953. He was accompanied by Roger Heim from Paris, a world authority on fungi, and Albert Hofmann of the Sandoz Laboratories in Basle, who had discovered LSD in 1938. They collected a number of fungi, including *Psilocybe caerulescens* var. *nigripes,* locally known as 'the mushroom of superior reason'. In 1956 James Moore, a chemist from the University of Delaware, arranged funding of $2,000 for a Wasson expedition on the condition that he could join it. This was agreed but, unbeknown to Wasson, Moore was a CIA operative whose aim was to obtain samples of hallucinogenic mushrooms in order to research their possible uses in developing mind-control drugs.

It is estimated that about nine indigenous groups in Oaxaca still use sacred mushrooms, including the Mazatecs, Zapotecs and Mixtecs. These peoples use a variety of mushrooms of the Agaric family, species of *Conocybe, Panaeolus, Psilocybe* and *Stropharia*, all of which contain the active substance psilocybin(e). Researchers at the Sandoz Laboratories isolated psilocybin(e) and psilocin(e) from *Psilocybe mexicana* in 1958. Hofmann noted the similarities between 'magic mushroom' hallucinations and LSD experiences. Among the effects of the mushrooms are auditory and visual hallucinations, alteration of time perception, emotional instability, hilarity and the inability to concentrate. No side effects – such as nausea – were noted, although some experimental subjects reported depression as the effects wore off.

Pilgrims of the peyote

The word peyote is derived from the Aztec *peyotl*, which means silk cocoon or caterpillar's cocoon, a reference to the woolly centre of this small and rather modest-looking cactus, *Lophophora williamsii*, and its variant *Lophophora diffusa*. These hallucinogenic plants, also known as 'mescal buttons', are among a number of psychoactive cacti of the New World that contain mescaline. Peyote grows in Texas and northern Mexico, in the environs of the Chihuahuan Desert. The traditional method of collecting it involves the removal of only that part of the cactus that appears above ground, leaving the taproot intact in order that new cacti may grow in its place. Hedonistic seekers of the plant have recently threatened its survival in some areas by uprooting it in its entirety. The Huichol Indians of Mexico, on the other hand, perceive their own search for peyote as a religious pilgrimage. Such quests involve a considerable number of participants and are accompanied by much ceremonial activity. The discovery of cacti with five ribs (i.e. parts) is deemed particularly auspicious, as this number is sacred among the Huichol and symbolises completion. Furst and La Barre, two anthropologists who have independently studied the use of peyote, believe that the rites of the Huichol preserve practices dating from before the Spanish conquest.

Sahagún states that both the Toltecs and Chichimecas had probably been using peyote for hundreds of years. The Inquisition arrived in Mexico from Spain in 1571 and soon began to suppress the use of peyote, describing its consumption as the work of the Devil. In seeking to outlaw peyote they actually denied that it had any inherent psychoactive properties. The following extract from an Inquisition document of 1620 has been translated by Irving Leonard:

> Inasmuch as the use of the herb or root called Peyote has been
> introduced into these Provinces for the purpose of detecting thefts, or
> divining other happenings, and of foretelling future events, it is an act
> of superstition condemned as opposed to the purity and integrity of
> our Holy Catholic Faith. This is certain because neither the said herb
> nor any other can possess the virtue or inherent quality of producing
> the effects claimed, nor can any cause the mental images, fantasies
> and hallucinations on which the above stated divinations are based.
> In these latter are plainly perceived the suggestion and intervention
> of the Devil, the real author of this vice, who first avails himself of
> the natural credulity of the Indians and their tendency to idolatry, and
> later strikes down many other persons too little disposed to fear God
> and of very little faith.[6]

Despite such attempts to uproot the cultural values of the indigenous societies, the task was to prove too much even for the Inquisition, and an uneasy compromise resulted. In 1692 the Coahuila Indians set up a mission named El Santo de Jesus Peyotes where cacti were sanctified at the altar. The folklore of the Mexican Indians included belief in a patron saint named El Santo Niño de Peyotl, who, it was said, could sometimes be seen among the plants of which he was guardian. Numerous instances of the tenacity of peyote-related beliefs in the Christian era could be cited.

The diffusion of the peyote cult among the North American Indian population is a complex subject. Not all groups embraced the new intoxicant as it weaved its way through Texas and across the Plains. The earliest reliable reference to the use of peyote north of the Mexican border dates from 1760. By the 1880s it was firmly established among the Kiowa and Comanche, who developed their own distinctive peyote ceremonies. Despite opposition from Christian missionaries – comparable to that inflicted on the Mexican Indians in earlier times – there are, even today, many communities in which peyote plays a central role. An estimate made in the 1970s suggested that the inter-cultural Native American Church (which combines Christian-based moral values with a peyote cult) had some 250,000 members in the United States and Canada.

The missionaries' insensitivity towards the reverential attitude of some native Americans to peyote is echoed in the activities of some scholars. Åke Hultkrantz, a Swedish specialist on North American Indian religions, was a participant at a peyote rite among the Shoshoni people of Wyoming in 1948. As he was a guest, Hultkrantz was offered peyote. Instead of consuming it as his hosts expected, he surreptitiously attempted to retain it for 'scientific purposes'. Criticising Hultkrantz both for his lack of respect towards the Shoshoni and for his clinical view of fieldwork participation, the anthropologist H. P. Duerr scathingly writes:

> To think that his Indian hosts allowed him to participate in a sacred ceremony, and the professor had nothing more urgent to do than to 'smuggle away' some of the drug, presumably to have it analyzed in the laboratory![7]

Dobkin de Rios describes Anthony Wallace's experimental work on the effects of peyote on whites and North American Indians in 1959. Wallace found that these two distinct groups reacted in radically different ways to peyote intoxication. The white subjects experienced extreme shifts of mood from depression and anxiety to euphoria, whilst the Indian subjects showed stability of mood accompanied by feelings of religious reverence. That cultural expectations and background can colour the contents of altered states of consciousness is beyond question, but one should be careful not to draw too simple a contrast between the peyote experiences of the two groups. As I have already stated, not all Indian groups who came into contact with peyote developed a cult in its honour. Even some of those who did had traumatic experiences in the initial stage of consuming this powerful plant. Among the Apaches of the Mescalero Indian Reservation, for example, shamans were considered to be a spiritual élite with special access to the supernatural realm. The arrival of peyote around 1870 disrupted this traditional position of privilege. Visions began to be experienced by participants in peyote ceremonies, and a conflict of interests arose in the community as a result of the incompatibility of these group meetings with the shamanic tradition. Peyote began to be perceived as intrinsically evil and its hallucinatory effects, far from being considered sacred revelations, as they were in some other Indian communities, were rejected as delusions.

The story of John Rave, a Winnebago Indian, further illustrates the dramatic effects of peyote on inexperienced users. Rave was born in the 1860s at a time when the Winnebago were suffering from the effects of forced relocation far from their original homeland. This movement resulted in their traditional economic and social organisation being severely disrupted, although their ritual and religious life remained fairly intact. As a youth Rave had passed through puberty rites involving fasting, but had not achieved membership of the most important ritual society, the Medicine Rite. Details of his early adult life were collected from informants and from Rave himself by the distinguished anthropologist Paul Radin. Rave, it seems, was a heavy drinker and had a string of broken marriages to his name. He had travelled widely and worked for a time in a circus, which seems to have taken him to Europe. In his own words, his heart was filled with 'murderous thoughts'. He was later to say:

> Today I know that I was in that condition because some evil spirit possessed me. I was suffering from a disease. I even desired to kill myself. I did not care to live. This feeling too, was caused by this evil spirit living within me.
>
> Then I ate this medicine (peyote) and everything changed. The brother and sister whom I wanted to kill, to them I now became deeply attached. I wanted them to live. This, the medicine had accomplished for me.[8]

Rave's personal transformation, precipitated by peyote, was a traumatic one. Unlike the puberty rites of his youth there was no clear cultural framework in which to place his peyote visions. Having alienated himself from his own traditions by his travelling and his moral turmoil, and not yet having embraced Christianity, he was in a marginal state and his initial use of peyote reflects this. His first experience of the 'medicine' caused him great anxiety and he began to regret having taken it, believing it would kill him. But by the next day he was able to laugh off his experience of the previous night. It was during his second session of eating peyote that important visions were revealed to him:

> Suddenly I saw a large snake. I was very much frightened. Then another snake (appeared) and came crawling over me. 'O my! Where are these coming from?' Then I felt something behind me and I looked around me and I saw a snake about to swallow me completely. It had legs and arms and a long tail and the end of its tail was like a spear. 'O my, O my! Now I am surely going to die,' I thought.
>
> Then I looked around again and there in a different place, I saw a man with horns and long claws and with a spear in his hand. He jumped toward me so I threw myself on the ground. He missed me. Then I looked back at him and he appeared to be going back. Yet it seemed to me nevertheless that he was directing his spear at me. Again I threw myself on the ground and again he missed me. Yet there seemed to be no possible escape for me.
>
> Then, suddenly the thought ran through me 'Perhaps – yes, it is this peyote that is doing this to me?
>
> Help me, O medicine, help me! It is you who are doing this! You are holy. It is not these fear-inspiring visions that are causing this!
>
> I should have known that you were doing this! Help me!' Then my suffering stopped.
>
> 'As long as the earth shall last, so long will I make use of you.'[9]

Following these experiences Rave continued to use peyote and attained visions of God. Radin, in his analysis of Rave's descriptions, remarks that the appearance of the snake seems to be related to its role in Winnebago tradition as a symbol of death. Although Rave was fearful of the snake, it did not actually seek to attack him, whereas the horned man (i.e. the Devil) did. It was only by calling on the protection of peyote and then receiving subsequent visions of God that Rave was able to overcome his own inner demon and reform himself. It can be seen, in this case, how peyote first magnified Rave's inner state of conflict and then aided him in overcoming it. Having taken up the Peyote Religion he returned to the Winnebago community to persuade others to eat it. Those that were converted to the new cult soon gave up the traditional clan ceremonies and the Medicine

Rite. Other, more conservative, people scorned the use of the new intoxicant and dissension and discord arose even within families. It seems that the cultural conflict that ensued was not as easy to resolve as the psychological conflict of John Rave.

Pipes of peace and commerce

Tobacco was undoubtedly the most commonly used of all psychoactive plants in native America. The antiquity of its use is proved by the abundant finds of pipes and related artefacts at prehistoric sites. The spread of agriculture from Mexico into the American south-west led to the growing of tobacco alongside the cultivation of the staples maize, squash and beans. Tobacco smoking was particularly important to the cultures that inhabited the Mississippi, Missouri and Ohio valleys from the first millennium BC (known collectively as the Woodlands tradition). Stone pipes have been found in burial mounds belonging to the culture of the Hopewell people (100 BC–AD 200). The site of Mound City, excavated in the mid-nineteenth century, was particularly rich in such finds. Mound 8 became known as the 'Mound of Pipes' after the discovery of some 200 of these artefacts. Most of them were carved in the form of animals, with birds (see fig. 20), amphibians and wild cats being among the commonest shapes. As Jonathan King writes,

> These pipes are undoubtedly the finest naturalistic carvings of
> prehistoric North America but their exact meaning and use will

20 Hopewell stone pipe from the site of Mound City, Ohio, carved in the shape of a bird eating a fish, 100 BC–AD 200. London, Museum of Mankind, W. Blackmore Collection.

always remain unclear. It seems probable, by analogy with more recent cultures, that the animals carved on each one represent a symbol of a spirit personal to a particular human being or his family or clan. In the historical period among the Algonquian-speaking peoples of the Eastern Woodlands an individual might dream of an animal whose spirit would then protect him throughout the rest of his life.[10]

Equally remarkable was the discovery of another type of Hopewell pipe which weighed several pounds and was probably used communally at special gatherings. Similar large stone pipes have been found at sites belonging to the Mississippi tradition (AD 700–1700). By historical times tobacco smoking was a widespread custom and played an important role both in the communities which cultivated it themselves and in those which relied on European traders and other Indian groups for their supplies. It was particularly important as a means of communing with the spiritual world and, since supernatural aid was invoked at the making of treaties, it became an integral part of the peace process. In order to express the communal nature of such covenants a single pipe would often be shared by the parties involved.

Among the Karuk Indians of California tobacco was seen as a heritage deriving from the gods themselves. Its use was largely restricted to adult men, although smoking by youths and medicine women was tolerated. The Karuk were not farmers, but nevertheless chose to cultivate tobacco in order to produce stronger strains than were available in the wild. They made their pipes from a variety of woods, including arrowhead, which was favoured because it has a natural hole which needs only to have its pith pushed out to make a perfect pipe-stem. Beetle larvae were often found by the Karuk in their stocks of dried salmon and they put these little creatures to work boring out the pith. The pipe maker would first fashion the bowl whilst the wood was still green and then imprison the grub inside it. The only alternative to death for the grub was to tunnel its way through the pith and, if it was successful in boring through to the other end, it both saved its own skin and provided its Indian master with a finished pipe.

The inhabitants of those areas in which tobacco was in short supply chose to smoke other plants rather than rely solely on trading with European settlers and other Indian groups. Species of *Lobelia* were smoked by the Cherokee, particularly for alleviating the symptoms of various respiratory disorders such as asthma and bronchitis. These species are known to act on the central nervous system and their effects are probably due to the active ingredient lobeline. The yellow flowers of the Scotch broom (*Genista canariensis*) were used by the Yaqui shamans of New Mexico for their psychoactive properties. Once picked, the flowers were stored for ten days in a sealed bottle. They were then dried and smoked in the form of cigarettes. The shamans would experience a marked increase in intellectual clarity and a more vivid perception of colours, whilst their overall consciousness remained unimpaired. The peoples of Alaska and Canada, whose environment precluded the development of agriculture to any significant extent, were in many cases introduced to tobacco by white explorers, fur traders and officials. They soon became habitual users but, owing to the shortage of ready supplies, they often mixed their tobacco with more available smoking materials. Such blends were called *kinnikinnik* by the Algonquian-speaking peoples (deriving from a word meaning 'mixed') and *larb* amongst the Western hunters.

When tobacco smoking was introduced into the native communities of the North-West Coast of Canada in the eighteenth and nineteenth centuries the traditional motifs which adorned their spectacular masks and totem-poles were soon used to develop a distinctive style of pipe decoration. Many of the pipes were made of argillite, a soft and easily worked stone which was found mainly on the Queen Charlotte Islands, the home of the Haida Indians. The main argillite mine was at a place called Slatechuck Mountain and the Skidegate Eagle clan had exclusive rights to extract it. From the middle of the nineteenth century the Haida began to design pipes incorporating European subjects such as sailors, ships' wheels and Western houses. This trend towards modifying traditional styles to make them more acceptable trade items was also followed by the Inuit, who included Western ships among the designs on their marine ivory pipes (usually made of walrus tusk). This tale of tobacco has a strange twist, for the Haida pipes with their depictions of Western sailors were based on European clay pipes which, in turn, stem from Indian originals acquired by the seafarers who first discovered the New World.

Five
. . . .
The Alchemists of Afek

> Mountain Ok cosmologists construct a model of complex and
> hidden systems of circulating substances in life forms, a kind of
> comprehensive physiology or *alchemy of life forms* animating the
> world around them.
>
> Fredrik Barth, *Cosmologies in the Making*

New Guinea has been described as the 'last unknown' and some remote
communities in its mountainous interior have only recently been contacted
by the outside world. It was not until the early 1960s that the importance
of hallucinogenic fungi in these communities began to be appreciated by
anthropologists and other Western observers. This interest was prompted,
in part, through the publication of an article in the anthropology journal
Oceania in which Marie Reay described 'mushroom madness' among the
Kuma people of the Wahgi Valley in the Western Highlands of New Guinea.
Although taken without ceremony, the mushrooms, or *nonda* as they are
called by the Kuma, were the catalyst for a saturnalia in which both male
and female consumers would act in ways entirely at odds with normal social
behaviour. Under their influence male violence – which in normal life was
directed at those outside the clan – was turned inwards: men attempted to
burn down the dwellings of their near kin. Married women, whose sexuality
was usually restrained, became lascivious and relived the sexual freedom
of their unmarried years.

In seeking to explain this 'institutionalised deviance', as she called it, Reay
was unclear whether the *nonda* were actually psychoactive species. She
revisited the Wahgi region for a three-week period in 1963, this time
accompanied by the eminent mycologists Roger Heim and R. G. Wasson.
Heim and Wasson identified the mushrooms in question as various species
of *Boletus* and a species of *Russula*, but were sceptical of their hallucinogenic

82

properties. Consequently they sought to explain the 'mushroom madness' by social and psychological factors rather than seeing it as genuine intoxication. Heim did, however, discover that two psychoactive *Psilocybe* species grew in Kuma country, although he claimed that they were not utilised by the local people. Emboden, noting the brevity of Heim and Wasson's field trip, suggests that their information was probably far from complete and that their conclusion

> assumes that the anthropologist and ethnobotanist going into a remote
> area will be given full information of an accurate nature by their
> informants concerning plants that they believe to be of a magical
> nature. I believe that such a presumption is untenable ... it seems
> unlikely that given the broad use of mushrooms, the presence of
> *Psilocybe* with its potent intoxicating psilocin and psilocybin would
> be ignored by native inhabitants only to be discovered by a non-native
> visiting the area.[1]

Harold Nelson, who in 1967 and 1968 conducted research among the Kiambi, another New Guinea community using fungi in a similar fashion to the Kuma, believed that the effects of the 'mushroom madness' he witnessed must, at least in part, have been caused by psychoactive species. Numerous Kiambi informants told Nelson that certain mushrooms caused a temporary psychosis that could continue to plague the consumer for a number of weeks. In some such cases the affected person would be bound with ropes and have the madness sweated out of him by the fireside, or might be thrown into cold water in order to bring him back to a state of normality. That both the Kuma and Kiambi themselves attribute the altered states of consciousness to the mushrooms casts serious doubt on the view held by Reay, Heim and Wasson that the phenomena are to be explained away by social and psychological factors alone. It is known that in many New Guinea societies much cultural information is jealously guarded by highly initiated men, even from the majority of members of their own communities. Since magical plants are part of this esoteric lore it should not come as a surprise that the identity of psychoactive species may be shrouded in secrecy. That the 'alchemists' of New Guinea guard their preparations as closely as did their medieval counterparts in Europe is demonstrated by Fitz Poole's account of the highly systematic use of intoxicants among the Bimin-Kuskusmin, one of the Mountain Ok peoples of the West Sepik region of New Guinea.

The central corpus of Bimin-Kuskusmin lore is transmitted through male initiation rituals. At each of the twelve successive stages of this hierarchical organisation a higher level of esoteric teaching is imparted to the initiates. The whole cycle is orchestrated by elders belonging to the highest degrees who, having passed through all the lower ranks, attain a profound and detailed understanding of the entire system of ritual knowledge. Sacred plants (known as *waraang* or 'heart palpitations' on account of their physiological effects) play an integral role in the workings of the cult. Each stage of initiation involves the use of a particular substance; the higher the rank of the participant, the more potent the intoxicant which is administered to him. An individual is permitted to use both the sacred substance assigned to his present rank and those belonging to degrees he has already attained. On no account is he allowed to utilise the substances reserved for men of higher degree than himself. The sacred substances are thus ordered into a hierarchy that mirrors the social status of those permitted to consume them.

The plants which play the most central role in sacred life are ginger, tobacco and mushrooms. Each of these plants – unlike the majority of those known to the Bimin-Kuskusmin – is believed to possess its own spirit, which guides the initiate into a particular region of the ancestral underworld. Because of their magical properties their use is subject to restrictions, not only within the hierarchy of the initiation cult but also outside it in the wider society. They are taboo to children and in most cases to women, and they are generally collected or cultivated by males with the appropriate ritual authority. Magical practices accompany the tending of these species, and different rodents and small marsupials are sacrificed at the bases of the various plants in order to assist their growth and potency.

The origin of the male initiation cycle is attributed to the androgynous ancestral being Afek,[2] who by introducing his/her blood, semen and bone marrow into the sacred substances invested them with magical properties. The consumption of these plants allows access to occult knowledge which would otherwise remain hidden. The attainment of revelations by initiates ensures the continuity of the cult, signifying as it does contact with the ancestral world in general and Afek in particular. The archetypal act of Afek is reflected in the ritual preparations of the initiate, which involve the strengthening of his heart, semen and bone marrow before he takes his assigned substance. Other preparations include temporary abstention from the necessities of life (such as eating, drinking and sleeping) in order to distance the initiate from the everyday world and bring him closer to the realm of the dead, that is, the ancestral underworld to which the spirit of the sacred substance will transport him. The ritual avoidance of children, women and men of lesser degree is another aspect of the temporary alienation from ordinary social life that the initiate must undergo. Chanting, dancing and drumming also heighten his state of concentration, as does the painting of his face with designs including emblems of both his clan identity and ritual rank and symbols representing the spirits of his own person and those of the ancestors.

The individual is believed to have two spirits – the 'experiential self' spirit (approximating to our notion of 'individuality') and the 'social person' spirit, which is shaped by cultural training concerning male identity and ritual knowledge. During states of ecstatic trance the 'experiential self' spirit remains in the body whilst the 'social person' spirit travels out of the body and, helped by a guardian ancestor spirit, visits the ancestral underworld to learn the secrets of esoteric knowledge. The spirit within each of the sacred substances allows the initiate access to a particular meandering path which leads to a spirit bridge dividing this world from the next. If the candidate is successful in his spiritual journey he will reach that particular part of the underworld connected with the specific sacred substance of his degree. Although there are significant differences in the effects of the various substances, an underlying sequence of techniques for the journey to the underworld can be discerned. Firstly, by communing with the guardian and ancestral spirits the initiate goes into a state of trance. He then attempts to make his own 'social person' spirit harmonise with the 'social person' spirit of the particular sacred substance he is using. By periodically checking the throbbing of his temples he is able to divine when the two spirits have aligned. At this stage he completes his facial design with the symbol of the 'social person' spirit of the sacred substance: this announces his ability to control his own spirit sufficiently to proceed along the spirit path. Then, having passed across the spirit bridge, he arrives at the sacred underworld, where he witnesses ancestral rites and increases his wisdom and insight into the mysteries of the cosmos. The guardian spirits then bring his 'social person' spirit back to the land of the living, where it re-enters his body. After one or two days the initiate, having been fully restored to the everyday world, rejoins his community.

Each of the twelve altered states of consciousness that form the initiation cycle is seen as an ordeal, for the taking of the substances not only offers spiritual revelations but demonstrates the initiate's ability to control the experiences, which increase in intensity at each successive stage. The first ten degrees represent the stages of male initiation, whilst the eleventh and twelfth are the junior and senior grades of ritual eldership. Ginger is the sacred substance of the first three degrees, tobacco that of the next six, and mushrooms are the supreme intoxicant, consumed by those of the three highest degrees.

The first three degrees of initiation all take place in the clan cult house. The sacred relics which are kept in this building (ancestral skulls and bones of the cassowary bird) are covered up, as their magical potency is considered too powerful for the young novices. A ritual fire is lit and the initiates are given ginger to consume at the break of dawn. Although the particular preparations of ginger differ depending on the degree of initiation, in all three cases crushed ginger leaves are placed in the nostrils and pieces of ginger stem are eaten. The ginger causes burning sensations in the stomach, blurred vision, terrifying apparitions, auditory hallucinations, nausea, dizziness, dehydration, trembling and general disorientation. But, from the Bimin-Kuskusmin point of view, the particularly significant effects of the ginger are the onset of erratic perspiration coupled with the throbbing of the temple, neck and chest. These are seen as signs of the generation of 'inner heat' in the initiate's body. In addition to the effects of the ginger the novices have to endure painful welts that appear on their inner thighs as a result of being rubbed with stinging nettles. That ginger could induce radical shifts of consciousness may seem surprising, but when it is borne in mind that the novices are full of anxiety and expectation before the ritual commences, and have already fasted and endured other privations, its psychoactive power becomes more explicable. First-degree initiates have to abstain from food for one day and sleep for one night. Candidates for the second and third degrees fast for two days and abstain from sleep for one night, and are not allowed to drink water on the day preceding the rite.

All the initiation rituals that involve the use of sacred tobacco (*Nicotiana tabacum*) also take place within the clan cult house, but on these occasions the skulls and bones are open to view, since the ancestral forces which they embody are no longer dangerous to men of these ranks and are in fact seen as aiding the initiate's search for occult knowledge. The smoking of tobacco begins at dusk; inhalation and exhalation is slow at first but gradually the initiates breathe in the smoke deeply and keep it in their lungs for as long as they are able. After a smoking session the men go outside the cult house to wander around in the wind and rain until they are shivering with cold, then they return to the low fire which is burning indoors to begin another bout. The oscillation between fireside smoking and exposure to the elements may be repeated a number of times. The tobacco used in these rituals is distinguished from ordinary varieties largely by its place of growth. Fourth-

21 Interior of a cult house of the Baktaman people, neighbours of the Bimin-Kuskusmin of New Guinea. From Barth 1975, pl. 18.

and fifth-degree plants are grown at the periphery of the ritual gardens of the elders; the sixth- and seventh-degree plants at the centre of the same. The more sacred tobacco of the eighth and ninth degrees is cultivated in forest clearings near clan ossuary caves (where the bones of the ancestors lie). Bamboo pipes are used in the smoking rites of the fourth, fifth and sixth degrees, whilst pipes made from a species of *Piper* are used in the seventh, eighth and ninth. *Piper* wood is also used to make ritual torches and as such it is supposed to increase spiritual perception. The privations which initiates undergoing this set of rituals must endure are more intensive than those experienced by the novices of the lower degrees. The fourth and fifth degrees require a one-day fast and two nights without sleep; the sixth requires a day without water in addition; the seventh and eighth two days without food, one day without water and two nights without sleep; the ninth two days without either food or water and two nights without sleep.

Whilst both ginger and tobacco are consumed in the context of collective rituals involving a number of initiates, the mushroom use by the men undergoing the final three degrees is an individual affair and reflects their ritual aloofness from ordinary social life. All three mushroom rituals involve prolonged exposure to the elements, taking place as they do in the mountains, far removed from the community of men. It is considered particularly auspicious to find mushrooms growing in forest areas frequented by ancestral spirits and cassowaries. On discovering them, elders apply wild boar fat, cassowary faeces and human semen to the mushrooms in order to increase their magical efficacy before they are gathered for consumption. The mushrooms used in each successive ritual are said to be found at increasingly higher altitudes, the twelfth-degree species growing in the mountainous heights.

In all three rituals one or two of the respective mushrooms are crushed and eaten raw. They are taken at night along with 'cooling herbs' which alleviate dizziness and other side-effects caused by the fungi. The tenth-degree ritual takes place at the entrance to a clan ossuary cave, the initiate having prepared himself by abstaining from food and water for one day and sleep for three nights. The species of *Boletus [Tubiporus]* that he consumes gives him access to the spirit path leading to that region of the underworld where the secrets appropriate to his grade will be revealed. The eleventh degree, that of junior eldership, takes place further up the mountain under a pandanus tree in the clan forest. After three sleepless nights and two days without food or water, the initiate consumes species of *Heimiella* or *Russula*. The final grade, whereby a man attains senior eldership, takes place among the rocks on the mountain top itself after three nights without sleep and two days without water. He also fasts for three days before the ritual, but during this time he is permitted to eat cassowary faeces which, being closely associated with the 'social person' spirit of Afek, are believed to assist him on his quest for the final revelation. The mushrooms used by the adept – *Boletus [Tubiporus]* or *Psilocybe kumaenorum* (?) – are considered so powerful and dangerous that even if a senior elder were to eat them in any other context they would poison him.

The status of these New Guinea adepts in their own community cannot be overestimated:

> The revered ritual elders who use powerful 'twelfth-stage mushrooms' ... represent the pinnacle of entitlement, ritual strength, knowledge and power. Standing alone near karst holes in the wind, rain, thunder and lightning, with tiny fires flickering and frail drums answering the echoes of thunder and flashes of lightning, they identify with Afek, the ancestral source of all ritual knowledge. In the wider Bimin-Kuskusmin community, they are the legitimate repositories and creators of ritual knowledge, and command the highest degree of ancestral power. Their lone vigil in the mountains, their dangerous use of the most powerful mushrooms, their daring journey into the 'sacred time-place', and their access to sacred revelations demonstrates their knowledge and power and control of the [sacred substances] complex.[3]

It is these senior elders who, knowing the most esoteric teachings of their tradition as a result of having consumed each of the sacred substances in the hierarchy, are invested with the authority and insight to add their own individual subjective perceptions to the existing body of knowledge. Lower initiates do not play such a creative role, for only the adepts of the community are considered sufficiently learned to create wisely. Other Mountain Ok communities who are close neighbours of the Bimin-Kuskusmin have similar initiation cults (although without the stress on intoxicants as catalysts for revelatory experiences) in which the creative interpretation given to traditional knowledge is carried out by small groups of elders who 'could rightly think of themselves as the Renaissance giants of their society, masters of nearly the totality of their group's culture and controllers of all its sacred lore'.[4]

Six
· · · · · · ·
Lucifer's Garden

In the folk botany of medieval Europe many plants were given names linking them with the Devil. Usually this was due to some obvious feature such as their physical appearance or noxious smell. A few of these plants (such as belladonna and henbane) were hallucinogens and were said to be nurtured by the Devil. The tradition of ascribing Satanic qualities to hallucinogens was continued by the French poet Charles Baudelaire (1821–67), who saw the artificial paradises conjured up by hashish and other intoxicants as delusions of the Devil, alluring in their false light but ultimately 'flowers of evil'. Whilst the 'flower power' era of our own century presented psychedelics in a more positive light, the subsequent growth in the use of heroin, crack, demon dust (PCP) and solvents has meant a return to a more sinister portrayal of psychoactive substances in Western culture.

The flight of the witches

> One morning Fotis ran into my room, trembling with excitement, and told me that her mistress, having made no headway by ordinary means in her affair with the Boeotian, intended that night to become a bird and fly in at his bedroom window, and that I must make careful preparations if I wished to watch the performance.
>
> At twilight, she led me on tip-toe, very, very quietly, up the tower stairs to the door of the cock-loft, where she signed to me to peep through a chink. I obeyed, and watched Pamphilë first undress completely and then open a small cabinet containing several little boxes, one of which she opened. It contained an ointment which she worked about with her fingers and then smeared all over her body from the soles of her feet to the crown

of her head. After this she muttered a long charm to her lamp, and shook herself; and, as I watched, her limbs became gradually fledged with feathers, her arms changed into sturdy wings, her nose grew crooked and horny, her nails turned into talons, and soon there was no longer any doubt about it: Pamphilë had become an owl. She gave a querulous hoot and made a few little hopping flights until she was sure enough of her wings to glide off, away over the roof-tops.

Lucius Apuleius, *The Golden Ass*

This fanciful account from the second century A D demonstrates the antiquity of the use of the flying ointments or witches' salves that feature so often in

22 A young Basque witch applying her flying ointment. Preparatory drawing for *Jeune femme nue dans une cuisine basque* by José G. de la Pena (1938). Bayonne, Musée Basque et de la Tradition Bayonnaise. From Robbins 1959, 41.

23 Witches travelling to a sabbat. The earliest printed picture of witches on a broomstick, from Ulrich Molitor, *De Lamiis* (1489). From Seligmann 1948, fig. 104.

medieval and later accounts of the practices of witchcraft. The flight of the witch was not, of course, literal, but was a hallucinatory experience induced by intoxicants in the ointment. Yet so vivid and powerful were the sensations caused by the drugs that many believed their experiences to be real. Travelling on a broomstick or in the form of a bird or other animal (see fig. 23), the witches would arrive at their sabbats, gatherings of witches, spirits and demons at which wild dancing and sexual orgies were reported to take place.

In many accounts the witch is said to rub the ointment all over her body (as in the case of Pamphilë).[1] There is some dispute as to just how effectively psychoactive alkaloids could have permeated through unbroken skin. A. J. Clark has suggested that the salves would work more efficiently if rubbed into scratches or the quick of the nails. However, there does not seem to be any evidence that the witches administered their ointments in that way. A more likely method is hinted at by Jordanes de Bergamo, writing in the 1470s:

> The vulgar believe, and the witches confess, that on certain days or nights they anoint a staff and ride on it to the appointed place or anoint themselves under the arms and in other hairy places . . . .[2]

The frequent sexual fantasies that accompanied the witches' flights may be partially explained by the manner in which the ointment was applied:

> The use of a staff or broom was undoubtedly more than a symbolic Freudian act, serving as an application for the atropine-containing plant to the sensitive vaginal membranes as well as providing the suggestion of riding on a steed, a typical illusion of the witches' ride to the Sabbat.[3]

Most accounts of flying ointments give the ingredients in too little detail for the effects on the user to be properly assessed. However, two early authors give reliable information. Weirus, a seventeenth-century doctor, gives the following three formulae of flying ointments: (1) parsley, water of aconite, poplar leaves, and soot; (2) water parsnip, sweet flag, cinquefoil, bat's blood, deadly nightshade, and oil; and (3) baby's fat, juice of water parsnip, aconite, cinquefoil, deadly nightshade and soot. Jean de Nynauld, in his *De la Lycan-thropie, Transformation, et Extase des Sorciers*, published in Paris in 1615, outlines three distinct types of ointment, each with a different effect. The first, used for going to the sabbat in one's imagination, is almost identical to Weirus' third formula (except that the fat of a child replaces the fat of a baby). The second, for riding on a broomstick and flying through the air, includes belladonna or alcohol or the consuming of a cat's brain. In order to turn into a beast (a process known as lycanthropy), parts of toads, serpents, hedgehogs and other animals must be mixed with human blood and various plants. The use of human fat and blood, cats' brains and the like must all have helped to induce a marginal psychological state in the witches who involved themselves in these dark forms of sorcery, but chemically the visions were induced by a small number of key plants, most of them belonging to the order *Solanaceae* (the potato family) – among them belladonna, henbane and the mandrake root.

The herbs of Saturn

Emboden has sketched the cloak of folklore in which belladonna is swathed:

Known as devil's herb, apples of Sodom, and deadly nightshade, this solanaceous plant is said to be tended by the devil himself, who nightly looks after this plant except on Walpurgis night, when he retires to the mountains to prepare for the witches' sabbath. At such a time the herb may metamorphose into an enchantress lovely to behold, but deadly in the viewing.[4]

Atropa belladonna is a noxious plant with dark purple berries. Its toxins (hyoscyamine and atropine) have a paralysing effect in small amounts but in large doses cause excitement of the central nervous system. Belladonna is rarely fatal except in excessive amounts: fourteen berries are said to be enough to cause death. The effects of belladonna intoxication are well known, as many doctors have had to treat children who have eaten the berries. In the initial stage of intoxication there is a state of excitation manifested as talkativeness, euphoria or hysteria; motor functions are also affected. In the second stage, the peak of the experience, there are hallucinations, delirium, manic seizures and nausea, giving way in the third stage to sleep. Delirium can also be produced transdermally, as is known from experiments in which belladonna plasters have been applied to the skin.

Henbane, another Saturnian herb, is admirably described by Gustav Schenk:

Black henbane, *Hyoscyamus niger*, grows on rubbish dumps and wherever the ground is covered with human garbage. We have only to look at this three feet tall plant with its grey leaves and yellowish flowers veined with purple to see that it is a typical poisonous plant. Sombre, luxuriant, sticky, evil-smelling and covered with close hairs, this sinister-looking plant seems to live exclusively on human refuse, on the corpses in the cemetery or the offal that lies around human dwellings. Black Henbane seems to suck up and retain within it all the poisonous matter from its habitat.[5]

Henbane's deadly reputation is a long one: it was used in ancient Greece as a poison. The great medieval scholar Albertus Magnus said that it was used by necromancers in the conjuration of demons, and this may be an allusion to the hallucinatory properties of the scopolamine in the plant. Schenk's own experience of henbane intoxication came from inhaling the smoke from burning seeds. He provides an interesting account of the powerful and strange effects:

94

My teeth were clenched, and a dizzy rage took possession of me. I know that I trembled with horror; but I also know that I was permeated by a peculiar sense of well-being connected with the crazy sensation that my feet were growing lighter, expanding and breaking loose from my body. (This sensation of gradual body dissolution is typical of henbane poisoning.) Each part of my body seemed to be going off on its own. My head was growing independently larger, and I was seized with the fear that I was falling apart. At the same time I experienced an intoxicating sensation of flying.

The frightening certainty that my end was near through the dissolution of my body was counterbalanced by an animal joy in flight. I soared where my hallucinations – the clouds, the lowering sky, herds of beasts, falling leaves which were quite unlike any ordinary leaves, billowing streamers of steam and rivers of molten metal – were swirling along.[6]

Aconite (*Aconitum napellus* – monk's hood or wolf's bane) is another poisonous plant which was used in antiquity. It was a favourite of professional poisoners in the Roman Empire and as such it was illegal to cultivate it, on pain of death. It is very poisonous indeed: the root contains about 0.4 per cent of the alkaloid aconitine, one-fifteenth of a grain of which is a lethal dose. Concerning its role in the witches' ointments, aconite has no apparent hallucinogenic qualities but may slow the heart rate and make it irregular, and, in sufficient doses, stop it altogether.

Hemlock (*Conium maculatum*) is a poisonous plant with small white flowers and a purple-spotted stem. Clark believed that the parsley mentioned in some of the old recipes for flying ointment was in fact a reference to the hemlock plant, which it resembles in appearance. (However, it is also possible, at least in some of the formulae in question, that parsley itself was meant. Emboden has pointed out that in European plant lore parsley has long been associated with the Devil, and researches into oils extracted from it indicate that it has amphetamine-like qualities.) Hemlock produces delirium and excitement and is also used as a powerful sedative, but its claim to fame is as a poison: Socrates himself was put to death, it is said, by hemlock. In fatal doses the effects are a gradual paralysis of motor functions and eventual paralysis of the respiratory system.

The swelter'd venom of the toad

Along with the black cat, the animal most frequently thought of as a familiar of the European witch is undoubtedly the toad. Wasson notes:

> The unpleasant abuse heaped on the toad ... seems to have been a fruit of Christianity. In Old French *le bot* was a name for Satan, resorted to as an evasive term, a word derived from a Germanic root, meaning the club-footed one, or the splay-footed, or the limping one. (Among Satan's traditional attributes was a bad foot causing him to limp.) That same word *bot* was a designation also for the toad and the toadstool, constituting thus a sinister trinity linked together in verbal identity.[7]

Could this be a survival of knowledge of the hallucinogenic properties of the fly-agaric from distant pagan times? And if so, why is the toad so closely linked with both the fungus and the Devil? As noted in Chapter 4, the glands of the toad species found in South America contain hallucinogenic substances. Toad poisons have been utilised in other parts of the world too, from West Africa (for example, among the Fang people) to China. That the common European species (*Bufo agua*) is poisonous has been discovered when toads' legs have been eaten instead of those of its cousin the frog. The side-effects of this unfortunate culinary error include extreme irritation of the membranes of the eyes and nose. Two substances (known as glucosides) have been isolated from the secretions of this grey-brown toad – bufagin and bufotalin, both of which belong to the digitalis group. This group of drugs stimulates the heart, causing it to beat more strongly and regularly and so increasing the flow of blood. Two other similar glucosides – helleboreine and hellebrine – are found in the root of the black hellebore (*Helleborus niger*), another Luciferian herb found in the witches' cauldron.

The magic of the mandrake

Probably the most famous of all the plants used by witches and sorcerers is the mandrake (*Mandragora officinarum* Linn., or *Mandragora officinalis*), also called mandragora or Satan's Apple. There is disagreement among botanists as to just how the varieties of this plant should be classified – whether as sub-species, or as different species altogether. Whatever the eventual outcome of this taxonomic debate, all the varieties contain significant amounts of scopolamine, hyoscyamine, atropine and mandragorine (this last substance is sometimes called cuscohygrine). The effects of these alkaloids are numerous and explain its widespread use in medical and magical treatments. It is an hallucinogen, an hypnotic, a narcotic, a soporific and an aphrodisiac. It can also act as an emetic (i.e. it causes vomiting) and has anodyne qualities (i.e. it alleviates pain).

Although our main concern is to outline the role of the mandrake in Europe, it should be emphasised that the plant was also the subject of a vast body of magical and medical lore in many other civilisations. Mandrakes have been found in the tombs of ancient Egypt; in Genesis 30:14–16 we read of Rachel seeking the mandrake to overcome barrenness; among the Arabs it was used as a particularly virulent poison; and numerous other examples could be added to demonstrate the peculiar and prominent history of this plant. In early Europe the principal system by which plants were assigned medical and other properties was known as the 'doctrine of signatures'. Simply put, if an observable attribute of a plant (such as its colour, form, etc.) resembled some other natural or cultural phenomenon, then an occult relation was thought to exist between the two. In the case of the mandrake the thick, fleshy and sometimes forked roots (usually about a foot in length) suggested the body of a man or woman. From this striking resemblance of form it was thought that the mandrake root could cure all sorts of ailments and produce a host of magical results.

24 Mandrake root fashioned into the shape of two bearded old men. From Thompson 1934.

Francis Bacon (1561–1626) noted that the root was used by witches and charlatans to make 'ugly images'. Although some of the mandrake roots looked very like a little man (or homunculus), others did not grow in quite so spectacular a way. The demand for roots was very high (especially in the British Isles, where it did not grow) as they were believed to aid the fertility of women. Impostors and quacks would 'assist' the natural shape of the root by carving it into a more human-like form. In Germany the mannikins fashioned from the mandrake root were known as *alraun*. Fig. 24 shows an unusual *alraun*, consisting of two male figures with bearded faces, given to the Museum of the Royal College of Surgeons of England by one Charles Hatchett FRS (the specimen itself seems to have been a victim of the Blitz and only the sketch survives). Not only were natural mandrake roots carved into more striking shapes for selling them to the gullible, but the bryony root (*Bryonia diocia*) was often passed off as the mandrake itself. Emboden describes the ingenuity involved in this deception. The bryony was carved to resemble the mandrake, then drilled with small holes into which millet

25 Bryony root. Oxford, Pitt Rivers Museum.

seed was put. The root was buried until the grain sprouted, then dug up and dried, looking like a little hairy man. Sometimes the natural shape of the bryony was close enough to be mistaken for a mandrake. On 16 May 1916 a labourer of Headington, Oxford, presented the curator of the Pitt Rivers Museum with a 16-inch long bryony root (see fig. 25). He believed it to be a mandrake and valued it for its magical efficacy. The comparatively recent date of this gift clearly demonstrates the tenacity of rural beliefs as to the wonders of the mandrake.

The mandrake, which grows in stony and uncultivated places, was also believed to be found at the foot of the gallows. It was supposed to grow there as a result of the semen of the hanged man falling to the ground. As a consequence of this belief the mandrake was known in Germany as *Galgenmannlein*, or the 'little gallows man'. Because of its human-like qualities, much superstition surrounded the uprooting of the mandrake, which was believed to shriek when pulled out of the earth. As early as the second century AD dogs were used to pull up the plant. A hungry dog was tied to the mandrake and some meat or bread was put down for him, just out of reach. In his eagerness for the morsel the dog would stretch the cord and pull up the root. The root collector would wait nearby, stopping his ears lest he hear the shriek of the evil spirit guarding the mandrake. This curious belief of the shrieking mandrake may be explained by its use as an anaesthetic. A sponge was boiled in a concoction of mandrake root bark, wine, lettuce seed and mulberry leaves and then placed on the face of the patient. When the effects wore off, the patient, or 'mandragorite', awoke in a state of fear often accompanied by screaming. This fearful shrieking of the mandragorite became, by a strange twist of lore, associated with the actual plant itself.

The Old Man of the Mountains

> Sometimes, due to contrary winds, he turned around to light an
> Egyptian cigarette whose smoke rose in spirals similar to the
> bluish mountains that blurred in the distance in Italy.
>
> Guillaume Apollinaire, *The Poet Assassinated*

Marco Polo, the thirteenth-century merchant from Venice, travelled overland to China during the heyday of the Mongolian Empire, when Kublai Khan, the grandson of Genghis Khan, was on the throne. In 1273 he passed through

Persia and in his *Travels* describes the fortress of Alamut, the headquarters of a cult known as the Assassins. Although Marco Polo was not the first European to describe this Persian sect, his vivid portrayal of the machinations of its leader Aloeddin – the Old Man of the Mountains – was to grip the Western imagination in a way no other account had done. Marco Polo begins his tale thus:

> In a beautiful valley enclosed between two mountains, he [Aloeddin] had formed a luxurious garden, stored with every delicious fruit and every fragrant shrub that could be procured. Palaces of various sizes and forms were erected in different parts of the grounds, ornamental with works in gold, with paintings, and with furniture of rich silks. By means of small conduits contrived in these buildings, streams of wine, milk, honey, and some of pure water, were seen to flow in every direction. The inhabitants of these places were elegant and beautiful damsels, accomplished in the arts of singing, playing upon all sorts of musical instruments, dancing, and especially those of dalliance and amorous allurement.[8]

Aloeddin's purpose in creating this artificial paradise was to convince his followers that if they obeyed his will he would admit them to heaven. In this he was echoing Muhammad's promise to the Faithful that if they followed the way of Islam they would attain the enjoyments of paradisal bliss. In order that none could enter the gardens without his consent Aloeddin built an impregnable fortress at the entrance to the valley, the only way in being through a secret passage. From the surrounding communities the Old Man of the Mountains would select young men between the ages of 12 and 20 whom he believed would make good Assassins. He administered to them a potion which caused them to fall into a narcotic sleep, and whilst they were still in a stupor he had them taken to a pavilion in the gardens. Upon awakening, the youths believed themselves to have been transported to paradise itself and gratified their sensual desires with the food, drinks and young women provided for their pleasure by the unscrupulous Aloeddin. After a few days had passed in this idyllic setting the youths would be drugged again and abruptly cast out of paradise. When they awoke they were willing to follow any command they were given in order that they might return to paradise. Aloeddin would send his young Assassins out into the world to murder his enemies and they would happily die in the execution of their duty, believing that they would go straight back to heaven.

This portrayal of Aloeddin perched in his mountain eyrie plotting the downfall of enemy princes and potentates, bewitching as it is, has mixed historical value. Both Marco Polo and his informants seem to have made full use of poetic licence in embellishing the factual foundations of the story. Alamut is the site of an ancient castle in the heart of the Elburz Mountains in northern Iran. Legend has it that a local king, out hunting one day, let his eagle loose and it came to rest upon a high rock nearby. Realising the rock's strategic importance, the king ordered a castle to be built there, which he named Aluh Amut (i.e. Alamut) which meant in the local Daylami language 'the eagle's teaching'. This fortress site was taken over by the Nizari Ismaili leader Hasan-i Sabbah on Wednesday 4 September 1090, and from that date until his death thirty-five years later he never left it. He occupied himself with reading, writing and the administration of his political affairs. Even hostile accounts of this first Old Man of the Mountains describe him as learned in geometry, astronomy and magic.

By the time Aloeddin (Ala al-Din Muhammad) became leader of the sect in 1221 the library at Alamut was widely known as a centre for the dissemination of Ismaili learning. But the historians of the Sunni branch of Islam have nothing good to say of Aloeddin; they present him as a drunken madman whose excesses prompted his own closest advisors to assassinate him in order to preserve the sect from imminent collapse. After the demise of Aloeddin Alamut remained an Ismaili stronghold until it was finally laid to waste by the Mongols in 1256.

Understanding of the Assassins reached a more informed level in the West when in 1809 Silvestre de Sacy, the greatest Arabic scholar of the time, made public his findings based upon previously untapped Arabic sources. He demonstrated that the etymological root of the title Assassins was the Arabic *hashish*. On the basis of this discovery he asserted that this drug was used by Assassin leaders in the manner described by Marco Polo. Subsequent research, however, has cast doubt on this literal interpretation. Hashish was widely known throughout the Middle East, and the dubbing of the Ismailis with the epithet 'hashish-users' is more likely to have been an empty term of abuse: the use of the drug is mentioned neither in Ismaili sources nor in the more reliable of the Sunni accounts. But my present concern is to show how Marco Polo's account was to inspire the nineteenth-century French intelligentsia.

Around the time that Silvestre de Sacy was putting forward his argument that hashish was the intoxicant utilised by the Old Man of the Mountains, Napoleonic troops were returning home from the Egyptian campaigns with cannabis. This novel intoxicant came to the attention of Dr Jacques Joseph

Moreau of the Hôpital de Bicêtre, who was already experimenting with the use of psychoactive substances in treating mental illness. Moreau had made a study of medieval remedies for alleviating symptoms of insanity and found extracts of *Datura stramonium* (Jimson weed) particularly effective. In 1841 he began to use hashish in his experiments, administering it in the form of a resin. He wrote on the subject of hashish with his friend Théophile Gautier, a major literary figure of the Decadent movement, and these two men were the driving force behind the setting up of *Le Club des Haschischins* in 1844. The club counted among its other distinguished members the writer Gérard de Nerval and the painter Joseph Ferdinand Boissard. They would meet religiously once a month in the chic surroundings of the Hôtel Pinodan on the Ile St-Louis. The hired rooms were prepared with impeccable taste:

> Flickering lights, ceilings painted with mythological scenes, Venetian goblets, fine porcelain, velvet tapestries from Utrecht, and Egyptian chimeras, all provided elements of the phantasmagoria that was part and parcel of *Le Club*.[9]

The order was under the command of a 'sheikh' called the Prince of the Assassins. This role was played by Dr Moreau himself, who would distribute green hashish paste among the assembled 'Assassins'. As he gave out each spoonful from a crystal vase he would ceremonially announce that 'this will be deducted from your share in paradise'. By the time Boissard had introduced Charles Baudelaire into the ranks of the Assassins, *Le Club* had begun to hold meetings in the flat of the Parisian playboy Roger de Beauvoir. Baudelaire's experiences with the intoxicant led him to write *The Poem of Hashish*, first published in September 1858. This essay was translated into English in 1910 by Aleister Crowley as the third of four works in the series *The Herb Dangerous* to appear in his occult periodical *The Equinox*. *The Poem of Hashish* is still one of the most perceptive accounts of the use of this particular intoxicant, blending intellectual rigour and precision with poetic imagination.

For Baudelaire there was nothing miraculous about the effects of hashish; it merely exaggerated the natural disposition of the individual, whose physical and moral temperament would remain unaltered by its use. He likens it to a mirror in which the consumer perceives his or her own impressions and private thoughts in magnified form, but this mirror only reflects what is already there. Baudelaire also refers to it as an oracle, the too frequent consultation of which saps the strength of the will, the most precious of all human faculties. Hashish increases the ordinary capacities of imagination, but what it gives with one hand it takes away with the other: 'that is to say, it gives power of imagination and takes away the ability to profit by it'.[10] The images induced by hashish are no substitute for the authentic spiritual labours of poets and philosophers. Those who seek to by-pass such work by mistaking their egoistical dreams for real action are damned by Baudelaire as black magicians and practitioners of witchcraft, doomed to failure by their too frequent evocation of the 'disorderly demon' named hashish. In characteristic Decadent style, the poet asserts that

> The stimulant poisons are, in my opinion, not only the most terrible and surest means at the disposal of the Prince of Darkness for the recruitment and subjugation of deplorable humanity, but actually one of his most perfect embodiments.[11]

The pioneers of psychedelia

In the late 1880s Louis Lewin made an analysis of the properties of the peyote cactus, to which he gave the name *Anhalonium lewinii* (i.e. *Lophophora lewinii*). He regarded it as extremely toxic, comparable to strychnine, and made little of its hallucinogenic effects. Shortly afterwards James Moorey of the American Bureau of Ethnology reported his observations of mescal rites among the Kiowa Indians and in 1894 he brought back samples to Washington for testing. In the same year, another researcher, named Heffter, succeeded in isolating the most active alkaloid from *Lophophora* and called it mescaline. In 1898 Charles H. Thompson of the Missouri Botanical Gardens, having grown specimens of the supposedly distinct species *Lophophora lewinii* and *Lophophora williamsii*, concluded that the former was actually an unusual variant of the latter. Consequently Lewin's name was dropped, although the term *Anhalonium lewinii* continued to be used in some quarters when referring to peyote and its mescaline extracts.

The famous psychologist Havelock Ellis was one of the first Westerners to write about the psychoactive effects of mescal, in his article *A New Artificial Paradise*, published in 1898. On Good Friday 1896 he retired alone to his quiet rooms in the Temple district of London and between 2.30 and 4.30 in the afternoon swallowed three mescal buttons in a decoction. He then recorded the experience, which lasted some twenty-four hours. In both his account, and a similar one by Aldous Huxley some fifty years later, descriptions of inner lights and complex geometric shapes clearly refer to entoptic phenomena. Soon after taking the mescal Ellis felt a desire to close his eyes, and gradually hints of the hallucinations to come entered his inner field of vision. There was an intermittent flickering of light and shade, which then began to form more definite shapes. So many kaleidoscopic images were clustered together that he was unable to describe them adequately. Spectacular arrays of vivid jewels of gold, red and green moved before his eyes, and the air around him seemed to be permeated with a delicious perfume. At this stage the slight discomfort of the early part of the evening had subsided, save for a slight faintness and tremor of the hands. It became increasingly difficult to write down the experience as he could no longer control the movements of his pen and had to resort to jotting down notes with a pencil. The vivid shapes continued to appear, like 'gorgeous butterfly forms or endless folds of glistening, iridescent, fibrous wings of wonderful insects'. He also records perceptions of shimmering vortices and other complex geometric motifs typical of entoptic phenomena.

So impressed was Ellis with the aesthetic value of the experience that he gave mescal to the Irish poet W. B. Yeats. Yeats was a member of the Hermetic Order of the Golden Dawn, a society set up to practise ritual magic. Its membership was largely drawn from the ranks of the Masonic fraternity and Theosophical circles. Another member was Aleister Crowley, who was dubbed 'the wickedest man in the world' by the gutter press of the time; he and Yeats were to be on the opposite sides of a schism that split the Order. Crowley believed himself to be the first to introduce mescal into European artistic circles, yet this seems not to have been the case. He first took peyote in Mexico, presumably on his initial visit in 1900 as a climbing companion of the mountaineer Oscar Eckenstein. This was, of course, four years after Ellis's first encounter with mescal. Crowley states in a marginal note written in his own personal copy of the semi-autobiographical *Diary of a Drug Fiend* that he made many experiments on people with mescal from 1910 onwards. Among these guinea-pigs was Katherine Mansfield, who tried it at the Chelsea residence of the literary hostess Gwendoline Otter. Apparently it only made her feel sick and rather annoyed at the sight of a picture hanging askew on the wall. Crowley, with his intense magical interests, attempted to classify various intoxicating substances into a cabalistic framework owing much to the old doctrine of correspondences. The varied and brilliant colours that mescal consumption induces were considered by him to relate to the planet Mercury which, in the Western magical tradition, was associated with a variety of colours. Crowley wrote at some length on the effects of mescal in a manuscript which is still unpublished.[12]

Following Huxley's publication of his mescaline experiences in *The Doors of Perception* (1954) and the ensuing public interest generated by this work, R. C. Zaehner, Spalding Professor of Eastern Religions and Ethics at the University of Oxford, decided to experiment with mescaline himself. At 11.40 a.m. on 3 December 1955 Zaehner consumed 0.4 of a gram of mescaline along with half a tablet of dramamine (to prevent possible nausea) in his rooms at All Souls College. A psychologist and a psychical researcher were present both in his rooms and on his subsequent walk through the town and other colleges. Zaehner found the experience interesting and at times 'hilariously funny', but he did not share Huxley's view of it as a genuinely transcendent one and decided on moral grounds that the use of intoxicants was artificial and 'anti-religious'. In the following years Zaehner was to write various diatribes against the rise of the drug culture, and in the debate over the use of psychedelic drugs he was to oppose the views of Timothy Leary, the 'high priest of LSD'. In response to Zaehner Leary wrote in his *Politics of Ecstasy* (1970):

> The Oxford orientalist R.C. Zaehner, whose formalism is not always matched by his tolerance, has remarked that experience, when divorced from dogma, often leads to absurd and wholly irrational excesses. Like any statement of polarity, the opposite is equally true: dogma, when divorced from experience, often leads to absurd and wholly rational excesses.[13]

Yet Leary himself was as dogmatic as Zaehner, albeit in a radically different fashion. At the age of 30 Leary took his doctorate in clinical psychology at the University of Berkeley and was appointed Director of Psychological Research at the Kaiser Foundation Hospital in Oakland. He subsequently joined the Harvard University Center for Research in Personality. In August 1960 he took *Psilocybe* mushrooms, an experience he was to describe as a revelation; he began experimenting on himself, his associates and volunteer subjects with measured doses of psilocybin(e). When this became known to the Faculty in 1963 he was dismissed from his post. In the same year Leary set up the International Federation for Internal Freedom (IFIF) and the *Psychedelic Review*. In addition to articles on the political aspects of altered states of consciousness this magazine contained poetic and artistic accounts of drug experiences and papers by eminent scholars such as R. G. Wasson and Richard Schultes.

Leary believed that drugs were the religion of the twenty-first century and that to pursue the religious life without them was like studying astronomy with the naked eye in the age of the telescope. This rather naïve view is open to various criticisms. Firstly, although pharmacological and technological advances have made the isolation of psychoactive substances a reality, there is nothing modern about psychedelic experiences. As I have shown, their use in Palaeolithic times is probable (see Chapter 1) and their use in communities with fairly simple technologies is beyond doubt (see Chapter 4). Thus, what seemed new and revolutionary to Leary was well known in other societies. Moreover, it is not in the realm of psychedelic drugs that technology has caused a revolution, but rather in the extraction of opium alkaloids for use in heroin. The social effects of heroin addiction are far from the religion of the twenty-first century as envisaged by Leary. Furthermore, the use of any drugs (psychedelic or otherwise) does not make people spiritually or artistically creative. Most hallucinogenic experiences are as boring as most dreams when they are related to another person. Over a century before Leary's psychedelic literature Baudelaire had clarified the fact that hashish was no panacea to the struggling artist. The same may be said of hallucinogens. Leary's view of drugs as a cure-all now seems dated, although at the height of the 1960s it probably seemed rather original. Some of his slogans epitomise the euphoria of the 'flower power' era and its political aspirations: 'Drop Out. Turn On. Tune In', 'The Only Hope is Dope', 'Turn on the Pentagon', 'Blow the Eight Million Minds of New York City', and so on.

In his eagerness to muster support for his vision Leary praised a variety of authors whose experience of drugs was reflected in their writings. James Joyce was entirely miscast as the 'great psychedelic writer of the century'. More fittingly, the Beat writers (whose work from the late 1940s and the 1950s had become widely influential) were cited as members of the 'movement'. Alan Watts, the English writer on Eastern mysticism and other topics, was the 'smiling scholar of the acid age', whilst Allen Ginsberg, the major poet of the Beat era, was the 'walking encyclopedia of psychedelic lore' and the 'celestial clown'. William Burroughs (who, incidentally, has consistently disassociated himself from the role of 'Godfather of the Beats' so often pushed upon him) was described by Leary as the 'Buster Keaton of the movement. He was Mr Acid before LSD was invented. The soft-bodied answer to IBM. Unsmiling comic genius.'

Burroughs' first published novel, *Junkie* (1953), written in the style of the 'hard-boiled' detective novel, established him (albeit under a pseudonym) as a drug writer. Although most, if not all, of his novels include passages on drugs, his literary corpus cannot be reduced to this single theme. The painter Brion Gysin, who was a friend of Burroughs, developed a new literary

26 William Burroughs in search of *yajé* in the Colombian jungle, 1953. From Morgan 1988.

technique known as 'cut-up'. This involved juxtaposing a section of written text with another which had no previous connection with the first. Gysin also went on a 'pilgrimage' to Alamut, inspired by the poetic tradition of the Old Man of the Mountains. Burroughs was to develop both the cut-up technique and his own idiosyncratic vision of the Assassins organisation.

Burroughs travelled widely in search of new experiences and described himself as a 'cosmonaut of inner space'. One of these journeys is recorded in the short text *In Search of Yage* (i.e. *yajé*), written in 1953 and published with additional material by Burroughs and Ginsberg in 1963 as *The Yage Letters*. Burroughs' search for *yajé* led him on 25 January 1953 to the University of Bogotá in Colombia, where:

> In a vast dusty room full of plant specimens and the smell of formaldehyde, I saw a man looking for something he could not find with an air of refined annoyance.
>
> He caught my eye.
>
> 'Now what have they done with my cocoa specimens? It was a new species of wild cocoa. And what is this stuffed condor doing here on my table?'

> The man had a thin refined face, steel rimmed glasses, tweed coat and dark flannel trousers. Boston and Harvard unmistakeably. He introduced himself as Doctor Schindler. He was connected with a U.S. Agricultural Commission.[14]

This 'Doctor Schindler' was actually Richard Schultes, who had already established himself as an expert on the botany of psychoactive plants. Schultes showed Burroughs a dried specimen of the *yajé* vine and told him that although he had tried it himself he had seen no visions but only colours. Schultes thought its supposed telepathic qualities to be 'all imagination' but he did suggest an area in which his visitor was most likely to find the vine. Burroughs followed up this lead and found an old sorcerer (or *brujo*) willing to prepare it for him. The sorcerer and his apprentice drank some of the alcohol Burroughs had brought for them, but he himself abstained, wanting 'straight *yajé* kicks'. Having placed a bowl on a tripod in front of him, the sorcerer began to chant over it whilst shaking a small broom to whisk away evil spirits who might otherwise find their way into the concoction. He then scooped out a small amount of oily black liquid into a dirty red plastic cup and gave it to Burroughs, who drank it straight down. Within two minutes Burroughs was overtaken by dizziness and the hut began to spin. Blue flashes appeared before his eyes and the hut 'took on an archaic far-Pacific look with Easter Island heads carved in the support posts'. Paranoia set in and Burroughs believed the apprentice was lurking nearby with the intention of killing him. A violent attack of nausea made Burroughs collapse to the ground; 'larval beings passed before my eyes in a blue haze, each one giving an obscene, mocking squawk'. He later realised this squawking was the croaking of frogs. After some ten minutes of fumbling with numb fingers, he managed to find his barbiturates. These alleviated the symptoms and he fell into an uneasy sleep. The next morning he had recovered except for a feeling of lassitude and slight nausea. He paid off the sorcerer, who had seemingly failed to dispel the evil spirits from entering the drink, and walked back to town.

Liquid lead and demon dust

There is nothing new in the flow of substances originally developed for medical reasons into the shadowy world of drug abuse. Chloroform was once used for its hallucinogenic effects, but the physical debilitation that followed repeated indulgence made this a dangerous pastime. Ether was similarly abused for its power to conjure auditory and visual illusions (see fig. 1), and there are reports of individuals under its spell constructing their own personal paradise where, with the accompaniment of ethereal music, they engaged in erotic encounters with beautiful women. The memories of these phantasmic allurements often drove users to repeat their experiences at the cost of their health. Even the well-known poison arsenic found its way onto the dressing tables of actresses and prostitutes, who risked its toxic effects for its ability to freshen the complexion, make the hair shine and promote a voluptuous figure. The dangers of this vain quest are too obvious to require comment.

Long before the scourge of glue-sniffing became a matter of widespread public concern, instances of solvent abuse in the workplace were reported. Lewin records the case of a German bandage maker whose use of benzine in his profession extended into his private life. He became addicted to sniffing it and, in seeking out help, detailed the nature of its strange effects. He would hear the discordant singing of disembodied voices clashing with a cacophony of barrel-organ music, and red ants would seem to creep around all over his body as he witnessed the figures of animals and dwarves parading in front of him. Solvent abuse was given a temporary and ill-deserved glamour during the rise of the punk rock movement in the late 1970s, when one of the earliest fanzines (underground magazines) of the cult was called *Sniffin' Glue*. Easy access to this cheap and dangerous intoxicant fitted well into the punk anti-aesthetic with its rejection of the 'hippy' drugs hashish and LSD. Widespread abuse in many parts of the world has led to restrictions on the sale of solvents to minors.

In present-day Australia a wide variety of volatile substances are used by both Aboriginal and non-Aboriginal youngsters. Whilst the better-known solvents are used in urban areas, petrol sniffing is practised mainly in the remote Aboriginal communities of Western Australia, South Australia and the Northern Territory and has been the subject of a detailed study by Maggie Brady. It should be emphasised that only a very small minority is involved in this practice; indeed, it is estimated that only 2–3 per cent of the 10–25 age-group participate regularly. The whole issue of intoxicant abuse among the Australian Aborigines is a delicate one; recently, with the rise of Aboriginal rights groups, self-assertive attitudes towards problems of this kind have been voiced. Brady quotes Merv Gibson, an indigenous spokesman:

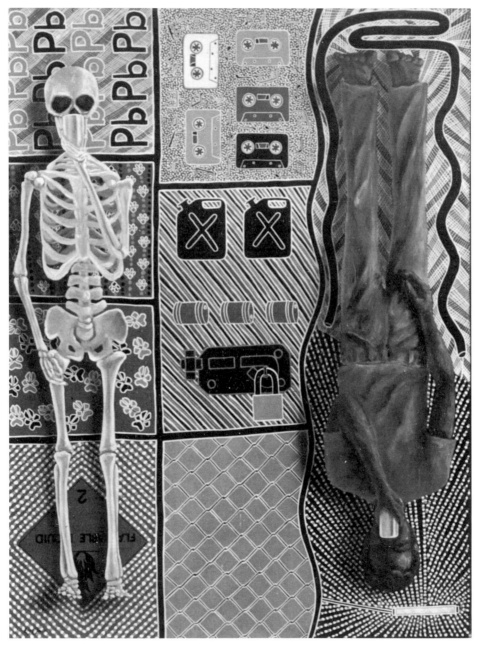

27 *Sniffer* (1986). Painting in acrylic on canvas by the Victorian Aboriginal artist Lin Onus in an Arnhem Land settlement. Reproduced by kind permission of the artist.

It is time to stop interpreting alcoholism as some kind of helpless result of culture clash. Rather we should see it for what it is: that is – the deliberate distortion of tradition for the sake of fulfilling an individual physical desire for alcohol. It is time to stop portraying the contemporary . . . alcoholic as a passive victim of colonisation. Rather we must consider how he has actively created his own problems.[15]

In comparison with the alcoholism that has plagued some Aboriginal communities, solvent abuse is a minor problem and there are no indications that petrol sniffing is likely to become endemic in the outback. As in Britain and America, media reports tend to exaggerate such issues out of all proportion. Nevertheless, petrol sniffing has caused more deaths among Aboriginal youths than any other single volatile substance. Whilst unleaded petrol is, of course, available in Australia, leaded fuel is still the norm in remote Aboriginal settlements. The inhalation of leaded petrol causes seizures, anorexia, vivid hallucinations and eventual brain damage (encephalopathy). Petrol contains, in addition to toxic levels of lead, other dangerous substances such as benzene and toluene. For reasons that are not yet clear, the habit is more prevalent in traditional communities whose main contact with whites was via missionary and government agencies. In those communities integrated into the cattle industry the practice is less common.

Petrol sniffers deliberately distance themselves from mainstream Aboriginal society. Their marginal state of identity is epitomised in the danger and thrill-seeking involved in sniffing sessions. In central and eastern Arnhem Land a number of petrol sniffing teenage gangs have arisen. Group identity is maintained both by the practice itself and by the names the gangs give themselves – the Skeletons, the German Rebels, Super Huns and Bad Brothers. Similar gangs exist among the Maoris and the Papuans, although they are not known to be involved in petrol abuse. In Papua New Guinea adolescent groups known as 'rascals' have developed (particularly in the capital Port Moresby) into organised criminal gangs such as the Rough Riders and the Harlem Lords.

The catalyst of the Los Angeles riots of 1992 was the general release of an amateur video showing a number of Los Angeles Police Department officers beating a black suspect. When they were brought to trial some of the officers in question attempted to justify their actions by claiming the man was high on PCP (which, in fact, he was not). They had previous experience of attempting to arrest PCP users whose extremely vicious behaviour, combined with a temporary superhuman strength, made them difficult to subdue. Before it reached non-medical users PCP (phencyclidine) was called Sernyl. In clinical tests exploring its potential use as a surgical anaesthetic for humans it was found to be unsuitable because of its violent side-effects. Being comparatively cheap and simple to make, PCP found its way into a variety of street drugs, and its popularity soon led to its manufacture in a pure form sold under a variety of street names including Angel Dust, Devil's Dust, Goon, Amoeba and Zombie. As well as being an anaesthetic, it causes hallucinations and has a variety of stimulating or sedating effects. Although it may induce a state of mild euphoria in some instances, PCP more often produces violent behaviour directed either against self or others. One man castrated himself whilst suffering delusions under its influence, and others have committed murders.

PCP is usually smoked, although other methods of consumption have been reported. Symptoms appear within minutes and the peak experience is reached within half an hour. The overall effects last for several hours, whilst full recovery may take a number of days. A fairly typical example of the behaviour of PCP users is the case of 17-year-old Martin L., as described by Ronald Siegel. After smoking a PCP cigarette he began smashing shop windows with karate-style kicks. When the police arrived he drew a butcher's knife and attacked them. They responded with baton blows but could not overwhelm him. Despite the force of the blows, Martin did not cry out; nor did he show any indication that he was tiring. Back-up was called and eventually six officers managed to handcuff him. On this particular occasion the handcuffs held, although other PCP users have been able to produce the 550 pounds of pressure necessary to break them.

Scientific and technical innovations of the nineteenth and twentieth centuries have made some of the active alkaloids found in the opium poppy and coca plant available in the highly potent forms of heroin, morphine and cocaine. The indigenous consumption of coca leaf extracts – a daily event in many communities (see Chapter 7) – was, and is, intimately related to Andean ritual and religion. It was the Catholic Church that first actively condemned its use, largely on account of its integral role in traditional spiritual life. More recently Western governments, perceiving its cultivation as the source of the problems of cocaine use in their own countries, have rekindled this view of coca as socially dangerous. Yet the evidence gathered by ethnobotanists, anthropologists and historians indicates that coca consumption has not caused any significant social problems in the area where it is traditionally used. This is in radical contrast to the use in Western societies of powder cocaine ('coke') and, more recently, rock cocaine ('crack').

Cocaine was developed in the 1880s, and Sigmund Freud described it as a medical panacea, a view shared by many of his contemporaries. The 'wonder drug' soon began to be taken for hedonistic purposes and its use continued to be widespread until the early 1930s, when the Prohibition of alcohol ended and amphetamines became generally available. The second wave of large-scale cocaine use in the United States began at the end of the 1960s, when many of those who had played an active role in the drug-influenced counter-culture graduated and began professional careers which gave them the financial means to buy cocaine. The use of the drug increased steadily but relatively slowly until about 1983, when a rapid rise in consumption took place. By 1986, the year of Ronald Reagan's war on drugs, the use of cocaine had reached epidemic proportions. Reagan's campaign was based on more than rhetoric and involved the sending of United States troops to Bolivia and elsewhere in attempts to curtail drug trafficking and coca cultivation. In order to protect their massive profits the Colombian cartels have developed considerable military strength and have recently begun to supervise the growing of opium poppies in an attempt to rival the Golden Triangle as the major exporter of heroin. This, it seems, is in response to demand by rock cocaine users, who have found that the after-effects of crack are alleviated by heroin.

In inner-city environments such as that of Puerto Rican Spanish Harlem drug use is rife. Marihuana, PCP, powder cocaine, crack, heroin and alcohol all play a role in daily life. Poverty and the lack of social opportunities encourage many individuals to give up degrading and poorly paid menial jobs for street careers as drug dealers. Philippe Bourgois, an anthropologist at San Francisco State University, has made a special study of the crack economy in Spanish Harlem and notes that, far from being alienated from mainstream values, the dealers pursue – albeit in their own fashion – many of the ideals of the American dream. The quest for upward mobility is manifested in their entrepreneurial aggression at the workplace – the streets and crack houses (often fronted by a *botanica* or herbal pharmacy). Both social status within the community of drug users and a sense of self-esteem may be gained by participation in the crack economy. One of Bourgois' main informants, on getting a job with his cousin selling crack, managed to give up his own crack habit for the less expensive and less dangerous powder cocaine and alcohol.

The crack trade in Spanish Harlem is based on terror, and the majority of victims are members of the community itself. Violent behaviour by the dealers helps to maintain their standing in a highly competitive business and any show of weakness under pressure is soon exploited by rivals. Owners of crack houses look for workers who have the nerve necessary to cope with armed hold-ups by robbers seeking cash and crack. The 'honour among thieves' code, which may be thought necessary in order to sustain business, was not cited by Bourgois' informants as a reason for trusting co-workers. It was rather the individual's reputation for ruthlessness that guaranteed his success; as one informant put it, 'my support network is me, myself and I.' Sometimes loyalty does not even extend to family, as the case of Indio illustrates. This individual,

> ... a particularly enterprising and ambitious young crack dealer who was aggressively carving out a new sales point, shot his brother in the spine and paralysed him for life while he was high on angel dust [PCP] in a battle over sales rights. His brother now works for him selling on crutches. Meanwhile, the shooting has cemented Indio's reputation and his workers are awesomely disciplined: 'If he shot his brother he'll shoot anyone'. Indio reaffirms this symbolically by periodically walking his turf with an oversized gold chain and name plate worth several thousand dollars hanging around his neck.[16]

Nearly half the users of crack in Spanish Harlem are estimated to be women and young girls, a considerable increase in comparison with female heroin use in the late 1970s. This higher female involvement mirrors the larger number of working-class Puerto Rican women in legitimate employment. The emancipation of women from the restrictions of homebound life has, for those who enter the crack culture, meant anything but freedom. Women have a generally low status on the streets and their need for the highly addictive crack draws many of them into prostitution. Often they do not even receive money, but sell their bodies directly in exchange for the drug.

Chemical purification has thus permitted the development of a highly addictive product to be exploited by unscrupulous criminal organisations. The phenomenon of crack abuse is a good example of what happens when a substance is removed from its traditional context: it is ironic that such a highly dangerous drug derives from the coca plant which, as a basically harmless stimulant, has been used for thousands of years in indigenous South American cultures.

Seven
· · · · · · ·
Stimulating Society

The difference between stimulants and other intoxicants is that the effects of stimulants do not, as a rule, preclude their use in the daily routine of social life. Although substances such as coca and kava are largely associated with ritualistic contexts, the consumption of stimulants is not normally restricted to important religious and ceremonial occasions, nor are they usually the prerogative of a chosen élite. Indeed, the fundamental role of these milder forms of intoxicant is essentially a communal one, namely that of stimulating sociability. The offering of tea, cigarettes, cola or betel to friends and strangers alike is a common form of extending hospitality, and qat parties provide a forum for social and business transactions. Nevertheless, differences in social status are maintained, sometimes by the order in which participants take the stimulant and often in the equipment that attends its consumption. Both the pretensions of the British middle class, embodied in porcelain tea sets, and the elaborate equipment of betel chewers hint at the vying for social status that goes on just below the surface of these apparently innocuous customs.

Coca, cola and qat

The coca plant (*Ethroxylum coca*) is a woody shrub that grows to a maximum height of about 2 metres (6ft 6in). Its golden-green leaves are harvested for their stimulating properties throughout the highland areas of Peru, Ecuador and Bolivia. The most common method of consumption is often called coca chewing, although this is not strictly correct as the leaves are in fact placed between the gum and cheek along with a lime paste. The function of the lime (which is similarly added to betel mixtures, see pp. 126–32 below) is to release some of the psychoactive alkaloids contained in the leaves. These alkaloids act directly on the central nervous system to alleviate hunger, thirst and fatigue. Emboden (1979) estimates that the average daily coca consumption of Indian users is about two ounces of dried leaves, in which the amount of cocaine is approximately 0.7 grains (less than 0.5 g). Such a small intake of cocaine is not addictive, and any attempt to equate the use of the coca leaf with the intoxication produced by purified cocaine is misguided. A. L. Spedding, an anthropologist who has worked among Bolivian coca cultivators, likens the effects of the leaf to those produced by a strong cup of coffee. The stimulating effects linger sufficiently to keep the user awake all night and, for this reason, coca is popular with long-distance lorry drivers. Although it is used in everyday contexts its fundamental role is in religious life, and important all-night rituals are conducted under its invigorating influence.

Coca use originated in Bolivia but it was under the Incas Mayta-Capac and Rocca in the thirteenth century AD that it was raised to the status of a sacred plant. This extolling of coca as a gift from the gods resulted in the rapid diffusion of both the plant itself and its ritualistic consumption. The Spanish invaders found a more cynical use for the coca plant, exploiting its stimulating effects to increase the work capacity of their Inca slaves, whom they forced to mine gold. The grim legacy of this colonial encounter is reflected today in the use of coca by poor Bolivian miners who risk life and limb to extract tin for the profit of foreign investors.

The coca plant is favoured by peasant cultivators of the Andes as it requires no irrigation, hardily resists drought and disease, and can be harvested three times a year. Yet the rapidly increasing use of cocaine in the Western world has prompted the United Nations to launch a coca eradication programme in Bolivia, and in 1989 local farmers were given $2,000 per hectare of coca uprooted. This sum was not an outright payment but a loan given partly in cash and partly in agricultural equipment. Coffee seedlings were also supplied, as the chosen replacement for coca. Such attempts to replace the traditional stimulant with crops such as coffee – supposedly a more acceptable product on the world market – cannot, however, be implemented without resulting in the eradication of the cultural values which are embodied in the indigenous plant.

Cola (kola) nuts are obtained from two species, *Cola nitada* and *Cola acuminata*, the former being the more common. The cola tree is 10–25 metres (33–82 ft) tall and its star-shaped fruits contain between three and twelve seeds, each the size of a chestnut and varying in colour from white to red. Trees bear nuts six to seven years from planting and can remain productive for several decades. The annual yield can be as high as 1,000 nuts per tree. Cola grows in the forest areas of West Africa, mainly in Senegal, Sierra

Leone, the Ivory Coast, Ghana and Nigeria. The most widespread method of consumption is simply to chew the nuts when they are fresh. In some areas seasonings such as ginger, malaguette pepper, salt and tobacco flowers are added. Traditionally cola does not seem to have been infused to make a beverage, but more recently the toasted and ground nut has been used as a coffee substitute. Cola nuts contain caffeine (2–4%), theobromine and kolatine, all of which contribute to its stimulating effects, including the alleviation of hunger and fatigue. According to the Zande people of the Zaïre–Sudan border region, it is also a remedy for hangovers! Cola nuts can be stored for up to a year, if kept in dark and damp conditions, but the kolatine breaks down if they are exposed to heat and light or if they become desiccated.

Although cola is harvested in the forest areas, the nuts are not, as a rule, consumed by the local communities but sold to the neighbouring peoples of the savannah. Cola has traditionally been popular with the Muslim inhabitants of the western savannah, who are restricted by their religion from using other intoxicants, but non-Muslims consume it in conjunction with alcoholic drinks. Coffee, tea and chewing tobacco are also used, but cola remains the stimulant *par excellence* of West Africa and is the subject of a long and rich tradition in this part of the world. As Sundström (1966) notes, it is significant that peoples living in areas of cola production have a very casual view of its consumption and lack a complex etiquette attendant on its use, whereas it is in those areas which import it that its social significance is most striking. This is partly because prestige attaches to those rich enough to consume conspicuous amounts of cola, particularly in times of shortage, signalling to others that the user has both the economic resources and the exchange connections necessary.

Traditional lore concerning cola suffuses the whole fabric of social and sexual life of its keenest consumers. It is claimed to be a stimulant to sexual activity in both sexes and a cure for male impotence. Women wear charms containing cola around their waists as a prophylactic measure against pregnancy. Acceptance of cola orally symbolises acceptance of a husband vaginally. Among the Bambara of the Niger river a bachelor seeking a marriage partner would send his prospective father-in-law ten white cola nuts. Should the receiver accept the man as worthy of his daughter's hand, he would reply with white nuts; were he to refuse, the answer would be a single red nut. The positive connotations of white nuts and the negative meaning of the red nuts were also part of the language of West African politics. In Sierra Leone a decision to fight was announced by placing two red nuts on a stone, while peace was made by placing the two halves of a white nut on a stone. A Nago proverb from Nigeria says:

> Anger brings the arrow from the quiver,
> soothing words a cola from the pocket.

Cola nuts also symbolised the prevailing social structure of the Nupe kingdom of Nigeria, where the king distributed different qualities of the nut among his various court officials, the grade of the cola corresponding to the recipient's place in the hierarchy.

Although the elaborate social symbolism connected with cola is limited to its African origins, the use of the nut is not. In the period 1870–80 the British, the French and the Americans began to experiment with cola as an ingredient in medical tonics. At the end of the nineteenth century it was mixed with coca and with soda to create the refreshment we now know as Coca-Cola. (Today, however, this product is made by purely chemical means and no longer contains either cola or coca. Other cola companies still use it, however, and about 100 tons are imported yearly into the United States.)

Qat (also spelt *khat, chat, ghat*) is the Arabic name for *Catha edulis*, an evergreen shrub or tree which grows up to 10 metres (33 ft) in height. It yields marketable leaves two to four years from planting and can continue to produce for up to fifty years. Although it grows in an area extending from South Africa to Turkestan, qat cultivation on a large scale is limited to south-west Arabia and north-east and east Africa. Institutionalised consumption on a significant level is restricted to the Republic of Yemen, Ethiopia, Somalia and Kenya. In the Yemen usually only the young leaves are chewed, whilst in Africa the tender bark and stem tips are also used.

In Somalia qat is used as a stimulant by a wide variety of occupational groups in order to increase work capacity and alertness. Both lorry drivers and judges use it to maintain their attention during long periods of continuous work. Religious men chew qat throughout extended sessions of prayer, and during the month of Ramadan (when it is the duty of Muslim believers to fast from dawn to dusk) it is used to alleviate hunger pangs. The regular consumption of qat has been seen as the cause of a variety of complaints including gastritis, constipation, insomnia, anorexia and the lowering of the sex drive. Such claims are difficult to substantiate, as the analysis of the effects of qat has been plagued with unfounded assumptions. It was at one time labelled as a narcotic, but research by the World Health Organisation has now established it as a non-narcotic and non-addictive drug. Yemenis, who have an intimate knowledge of the effects of qat, classify it with tea and coffee and not with stronger intoxicants such as hashish or alcohol. Early research identified the substance cathin as the principal stimulant in qat, but it has subsequently been shown that the primary active agent in the leaves is cathinone.

Ideally qat needs to be consumed within forty-eight hours of being picked, otherwise it begins to lose its stimulating qualities. In north-east Africa the expansion and modernisation of land and air communications has meant that the leaves can be transported more rapidly and thus to a larger number of potential consumers. The Somali authorities estimated that at the beginning of the 1980s some 200,000 of their people were involved in the production and exchange of qat. The government felt that this was a waste of both land and labour resources and as a consequence the stimulant was banned. The ban was enforced not only for economic reasons but also because qat was seen as a political and social threat. Much of the qat industry was conducted without government involvement and some of the con-

28 A qat party in Razih, Yemen, 1977. From Weir 1985, fig. 30.

siderable profits went towards funding opposition groups operating from bases outside the country.

The use of qat grew in urban areas of Somalia partly as a result of its popularity with migrant workers who, returning from Saudi Arabia during and after the oil boom of the 1970s, had the financial resources to purchase it. In response to the increasing demand, qat houses (*majlis*) were set up as meeting places for these new groups of consumers. Qat houses are usually owned by divorced or widowed women and tend to attract specific classes of customer: certain qat houses are frequented almost solely by truck drivers, others by civil servants, and so on. Qat sessions usually last at least three hours, and the chewing of the leaves is accompanied by the serving of tea, water and soft drinks as well as the smoking of cigarettes. Bearing in mind that some regular qat users meet on a daily basis, the interactions that take place at the *majlis* play an important part in shaping their social lives. Such gatherings go against the grain of the traditional patterns of Somali identity, which are centred on family and clan allegiance, and as such are viewed by more conservative elements as potentially subversive.

The financial prosperity resulting from the oil boom had similar effects on qat consumption in the Republic of Yemen. Up until the 1970s qat was used almost exclusively by a rich urban élite, but the rapid growth in its popularity among the *nouveaux riches* initiated a challenge to the traditional role of the qat party as a means of maintaining conservative values. Today qat parties provide the upwardly mobile with a forum in which new social networks can be formed, and ritualistic elements are incorporated into the seating order, which reflects the rank of each participant. These parties usually begin around 2 or 3 p.m. and continue until dusk:

> Yemenis divide the sequence of moods into three distinct phases. In the first they feel awake and alert, their thoughts are clarified, memories flow, loquaciousness increases, and communication and sense of community are enhanced; the second (*kayf*) is when the peak of communal understanding and well-being is reached, men feel in more harmony with themselves and others and may be transported to a more religious or philosophical plane of contemplation where countless projects seem attainable and problems soluble; and the third is characterised by temporary sadness and spiritual unease as the qat is finished, its effects wear off and the party draws to a close.[1]

Whilst these are the effects enjoyed by the majority of qat users, a significant number of individuals (including heavy users) do not experience *kayf*. Their reason for participating, it seems, is for the stimulating effect of the social occasion rather than that of the qat itself. Such behaviour emphasises the importance that should be placed on the social context in which a stimulant is used; any account which attempts to locate the source of stimulation in the plant alone fails in its appreciation of the strength of its cultural roots.

Stimulating beverages: coffee, cocoa and tea

In our own society the most socially acceptable stimulants are probably the beverages coffee, tea and cocoa. *Coffea arabica* is a shrub or small tree that grows up to 5 metres (16 ft) in height and yields a crop three to six years from planting, depending on local conditions. The tree can remain productive for up to forty years. It seems likely that its original home was the Ethiopian Highlands, and it was from here that plants were brought to Arabia around the sixth century A D and first domesticated. For a long time coffee was used as a food; it was only in the fifteenth century that a beverage was made from it. The berries of the coffee plant have two seeds which, when dried and processed, become the familiar coffee beans so widely consumed in our society. Often beans from different areas are combined to make the various blends available to the coffee drinker. The success of the blend depends on the quality of the beans, the care taken in the processing and the discernment of professional coffee tasters (see fig. 29).

Coffee was brought to England by Anthony Sherley in 1601. It was first known as *kahveh*; the spelling we now use universally was introduced soon afterwards by William Parry. Coffee was drunk as a social beverage in Balliol College, Oxford, in the 1630s, and Oxford opened its first coffee-house, the Angel, in 1650. The drink reached Paris in 1643 and soon caught on; the city had 250 coffee-houses by 1690 and 1,800 by 1782. The famous Parisian café society was by this time firmly rooted. Coffee-houses also spread to America, where Boston opened its first in 1689. The cultivation of coffee spread rapidly beyond the confines of north-east Africa and Arabia into other suitable areas with moist and hot climates and significant rainfall. The Dutch planted coffee in Java and Ceylon at the end of the seventeenth century, and in the following 100 years it spread to South America, which was to establish itself as the biggest coffee producer. The source of this rapid expansion into the New World was a single tree sent from Java to Amsterdam, where it was grown in the botanical garden:

29 A coffee taster sampling various blends.

Seeds from this tree were sent to Surinam in 1718; this led to plantings
in French Guiana and, eventually, to the establishment of the
enormous Brazilian coffee industry in 1727. A descendant of the
original tree in Amsterdam was sent in the Jardin des Plantes in Paris,
and this provided the seed for the French introduction of coffee into
the Caribbean island of Martinique in 1720. From these introductions,
coffee was spread throughout the New World. Even Hawaiian and
Philippine coffee trees are derived from the lonely tree in Amsterdam.
This is a striking illustration of the role played by botanical gardens
in the history of colonial (and later national) development in the
tropics. Coffee is now produced all around the world between the
tropics of Capricorn and Cancer.[2]

The physiological effects of coffee are due to caffeine and other alkaloids.
It is a well-known fact that it stimulates brain and heart activity, and it
has been used medically in cases of heart disease, asthma and barbiturate
poisoning. Excessive consumption of coffee can cause stomach complaints
and nervous problems, but fatal overdoses have not been reported.

The tree from which cocoa derives is native to the Amazon valley and was brought to Mexico in pre-Hispanic times. The Aztecs called it *chocolatl*, 'food of the gods', and Linnaeus translated this evocative title into Greek to give it the scientific name *Theobroma cacao*. Among the Aztecs the use of cocoa was an aristocratic privilege and this was reflected in the elaborate goblets of gold in which it was served and in the spoons of gold and tortoiseshell with which it was eaten.

Cocoa first came to the attention of Europeans when Hernando Cortés landed in Mexico in 1519. Among the human booty of conquest was a princess Doña Marina, who assured her lover Cortés that the drink was aphrodisiac. On returning to Spain in 1528 Cortés informed the emperor Charles V of his discovery. Use of cocoa spread to Flanders and Italy soon after 1605 and by the 1650s it was established in France and England both in the form of a drink and as a tablet or bar. Both drinking chocolate and chocolate bars are made from the roasted and de-husked beans. In the case of the drink the bulk of the natural oil is removed, whilst to make solid chocolate further oils are added. Sugar is an additional ingredient in both preparations. Analysis shows that the idea of cocoa being an aphrodisiac is unfounded. The active ingredient, theobromine, is a compound with effects similar to those of caffeine.

Most of the world's cocoa is produced in Nigeria and Ghana, where it was introduced during the colonial era. It was a recurring feature of colonial agriculture that major crops from one continent were transplanted to another, where the new plantations gradually outstripped the traditional growing areas. One reason for this was that many of the pests that plagued the native crops were absent in other regions of the world.

The tea plant is known to botanists as either *Camellia thea* or *Thea sinensis*. It grows well in tropical hill country and at lower elevations in sub-tropical areas. If left to grow naturally tea grows into a tree up to 10 metres (33 ft) tall, but when cultivated for its leaves it is kept down to the size of a shrub. It is native to China, India and neighbouring countries and is usually classified into two distinct groups, the large-leaved Indian types and the narrow-leaved Chinese variety. The former grow both in India itself and in Sri Lanka and constitute the lion's share of the world export market; although China produces even more, most of it is consumed domestically. Teas are also classified according to the methods of processing the leaves. Before it is fired (i.e. cured by heat) black tea is fermented by lightly crushing the leaves, a process that extracts tannins. Green tea is fired immediately, thus limiting the process of fermentation. Oolong tea leaves are partly oxidised before firing for a short time.

If consumed in moderation, tea is basically harmless. In extreme cases, such as that described by Lewin (1964) of a tea-addict who drank thirty cups a day, hallucinations and a host of other disturbing symptoms can occur. In the traditional lore of the Chinese, however, many beneficial effects are attributed to the drinking of tea. It is said to stimulate the thoughts and aid concentration, to increase the flow of blood around the body, to build up the body's resistance to disease, to prevent tooth decay and to promote longevity. Recent medical research in Japan has confirmed the first four of these claims but not – at least so far – the latter two.

Although China does not have an elaborate tea ceremony like that conducted in Japan, tea lore nevertheless permeates the culture. Various legends in China attribute the discovery of tea to a very early period, but it seems certain that it was known in the Three Kingdoms period (third century AD). By the Golden Age of Chinese high culture, the Tang Dynasty (AD 618–906) tea had attained a position of cultural prominence. Alongside elaborate and beautiful teapots, kettles and cups, tea was also an inspiration to poets. Lu Tung, a Tea Master from North China born at the end of the eighth century, wrote what is probably the most famous poem extolling the delights of tea. The eulogy is entitled 'Thanks to Imperial Censor Meng for his Gift of Freshly Picked Tea' and is translated by Blofeld as follows:

The first bowl sleekly moistened throat and lips;
The second banished all my loneliness;
The third expelled the dullness from my mind,
Sharpening inspiration gained from all the books I've read.
The fourth brought forth light perspiration,
Dispersing a lifetime's troubles through my pores.
The fifth bowl cleansed ev'ry atom of my being.
The sixth has made me kin to the Immortals.
The seventh is the utmost I can drink –
A light breeze issues from my armpits.

The connoisseurship of tea fanatics in Chinese culture is comparable to that of European wine lovers, as the marvellously evocative names of different brews attest: 'Sparrow's Tongue', 'Dragon's Well', 'Iron Goddess of Mercy', 'Old Man's Eyebrows', 'Drunken Concubine Yang' are just a few examples from this rich tradition.

As coffee was used by European monks for maintaining attention during long evenings of prayer, so too was tea drunk by both Taoist and Buddhist

30 Copper tea cauldrons used by Tibetan monks, photographed in Lhasa in the 1920s. Oxford, Pitt Rivers Museum, Bell Collection.

monks as an aid to meditation. It also played a major role in the religious life of the Buddhist monks of Tibet, where the tea was brewed in vast copper cauldrons (see fig. 30). More unusually, tea was given in large quantities to the horses and mules of Tibet to increase their capacity for work. Both Tibetan and Mongolian nomads habitually add butter or animal fat to their tea, and in Mongolia the inclusion of yak faeces has also been reported.

The various inhabitants of Turkestan (Uzbeks, Uighurs, Tajiks, Tatars, Kirghiz and Kazakhs) have long used both black and green tea. In Afghan Turkestan tea is consumed in two forms – as a beverage and as a kind of soup. Essential to the tea-houses of this region is the *samovar*, or tea-urn, first imported from Russia and then made locally. Both here and in Eastern Turkestan the tea-house itself is named after the urn, i.e. *samovar* and *samavar-xana* in the respective areas. *Samovars* are filled with water and charcoal and

125

in restaurants and tea-houses kept boiling all day. The customers would originally have been served with a porcelain teapot and a bowl without a handle. Teapots made by a porcelain factory set up in czarist Russia by an enterprising Englishman named Gardner are especially favoured, and in areas such as Nuristan confer informal social prestige and standing on account of their quality and their rarity in the remote regions of Central Asia. Porcelain teapots are often given as marriage gifts in contemporary Central Asia as it is believed that if poison enters the pot it will immediately break. They have thus become an emblem of security and good health. In Afghanistan porcelain began to give way to modern goods in the 1970s: cheap metal teapots were imported from the USSR and the Peoples' Republic of China and Duralex glasses and cups from the West.

In addition to tea proper, the inhabitants of the steppes of Western Turkestan drink a special mint tea derived from *Lagochilus inebrians*. This spiny shrub, which grows wild in the dry steppelands, is collected in October when it has no flowers. The stems are tied up in bundles and left to dry for some months. This process of drying actually increases the fragrance of the stems which are boiled to make the tea. The properties and effects of this mint and similar species are not yet fully understood, although Russian pharmacologists have isolated lagochiline, which is known to have sedative properties and which has also been used to treat allergies, skin complaints and haemorrhaging. Although the plant is reported to have hallucinogenic properties, no psychoactive substances which might induce visions have been found in it.

Betel chewing in Asia and Oceania

The habit of 'betel chewing' is practised by approximately one-tenth of the world's population. Users may be found throughout the betel plant's natural area of growth, from Tanzania and Madagascar in the west, across the Indian subcontinent and South-East Asia, and in the western Pacific islands as far as Tikopia. The term 'betel-nut' chewing is in fact something of a misnomer, as the nut in question is actually the seed of the areca palm (*Areca catechu*) which is mixed with slaked lime and wrapped in a leaf of the betel plant (*Piper betle*). The betel quid is placed between the tongue and cheek; some heavy users not content with daytime 'chewing' alone often keep it in their mouths whilst they sleep. Frequent use of the betel mixture causes a build-up of lime and other residues which blacken the teeth. In some traditional societies blackened teeth were a symbol of high social status; however, in

126

the Philippines today the term 'black teeth' has become an abusive term meaning illiterate.

There are nine identified active alkaloids in the areca nut, the most significant being arecoline which, when combined with lime, makes arecaidine. Arecaidine is a stimulant to the central nervous system and has nicotine-like properties. The chewing of betel increases the flow of tears, sweat and saliva. Copious amounts of red-coloured saliva are generated which, in South and South-East Asia, are ejected into spittoons. Betel produces a general feeling of well-being and good humour and suppresses hunger and fatigue. In general, consciousness remains unimpaired, although hallucinations have been reported by some consumers. Users say that it gives the breath a pleasant odour. Despite the fact that modern research into the properties of betel has found no supporting evidence, betel is widely believed to be an aphrodisiac. Indian sources affirm its role in the erotic life of the subcontinent, and in Melanesia it is chewed whilst making love. It has been suggested that there may be a link between betel chewing and oral cancer, but this has not been proved. Cases of the disease among chewers may, in fact, be due to the simultaneous use of tobacco rather than to any intrinsic quality of the betel mixture itself.

Archaeological evidence suggests that betel use originated in prehistoric South-East Asia. Remains of *Piper* seeds and areca have been discovered at the Spirit Cave site in north-west Thailand and are estimated to date from the period 7000–5500 BC. A similar find on the island of Timor in eastern Indonesia dates back to about 3000 BC. At the Duyong Cave site (2680 BC) on Palawan in the Philippines a male skeleton was discovered with betel-stained teeth, and beside it were a number of bivalve shells containing lime. The lack of any such early evidence of betel consumption in India suggests that the practice was diffused from South-East Asia around the beginning of the Christian era when references to it appear in the contemporary literature. Once established it became a significant pastime:

> In India betel [has] long been regarded as one of the eight *bhogas* or cardinal pleasures of life, along with unguents, incense, women, music, bed, food and flowers. Poets sang of it, scholars argued over it, but, most of all, everyone from the Emperor to the humblest agricultural labourer was chewing it.[3]

In its original homeland betel had an equally prominent position. Of particular interest is its role in marriage negotiation, which bears a striking resemblance to that of cola in West African communities. (see p. 117 above). The family of a young suitor seeking the hand of a girl in marriage offered her parents various presents including betel, acceptance of which signified agreement to the proposal. The use of the stimulants tea and coffee as an aid to contemplation and meditation among European, Tibetan and Chinese monks has already been noted, and betel performs a similar function among communities of Buddhist monks in Burma and Sri Lanka.

In both South and South-East Asia a variety of flavour enhancers are added to the three basic ingredients of the betel mixture. These include saffron, cloves, turmeric, syrup, melon seeds, cardamom, rosewater, tamarind, musk and ambergris. The consumption of betel is attended by elaborate sets of equipment which also serve to highlight the social status of their owners. These include containers for lime paste and betel leaf, mortars, spittoons, dishes and betel cutters (used to cut the areca nuts). The betel cutters are the most highly decorated items and their manufacture requires highly skilled craftsmanship. A detailed account of the diversity of regional styles, accompanied by lavish illustrations, may be found in Brownrigg 1991.

In neither mainland nor island Melanesia does there seem to have been any significant decline in betel use despite modernisation and the large-scale introduction of coffee, tobacco and other stimulants. In fact, recent improvements in road communications in Papua New Guinea have led to the commercialisation of betel and its introduction into parts of the interior where it was not traditionally consumed. In 1981 the authorities of the Western Highlands Province tried to impose a ban on its use on the grounds that it was keeping people from working their land. This and other attempts to suppress betel have had little success and today market traders throughout the country openly sell betel ingredients to an eager public. Alfred Gell's observations of life in Umeda village in the West Sepik District of Papua New Guinea show just how firmly rooted the social functions of betel chewing can be:

> The effect of chewing Areca with lime and betel is to produce a sensation of mild dissociation; an unwonted feeling of reduced gravity, a dulling of hunger and fatigue, and in addition a sharpening of visual acuity. In short, Areca induces a 'marginal' state of consciousness, putting the user slightly 'outside' himself. Areca is chewed routinely by all actors in rituals, as well as having a specific magical function, which I shall note.

> Areca-chewing and spitting red betel juice mediates ritual
> transitions . . . after contact with magical substances men smear their
> bodies with betel juice . . . which acts as a kind of magical 'disinfectant'.
> As well as removing pollution, betel-spit is used to impart magical
> power, for example to ritual masks, just before they are to be used.
> And it is used in various curing rituals, both by officiants and patients.
> It is not only such ritual transitions that chewing Areca mediates.
> Chewing is a part of daily life. The moments when Areca is chewed
> are precisely the points of transition in the course of the day: the early
> morning (as indispensable a pleasure as the first cigarette of the day)
> and at night, while relaxing in camp, and also before and after
> undertaking any task, going on an expedition etc.[4]

A picture thus emerges of betel use in both ritual activities and in daily routine, although it should be emphasised that betel consumption is not, in the vast majority of cases, the focus of rituals (unlike kava: see pp. 132–5 below) but merely a component element in their execution. Again in contrast to kava, there is little in the ethnographic accounts indicating restricted or élite access to the stimulant. It is informally and regularly used by all age groups (including children), both sexes, 'Christians' and 'pagans', initiates and non-initiates. The offering of betel to both strangers and intimates is a sign of goodwill and hospitality, like our serving guests with tea or coffee.

Although the atmosphere surrounding the consumption of betel is informal and relaxed, the paraphernalia used in its preparation often indicates the social standing of users. One of the main art forms of the Massim area of East New Guinea is the highly decorated spatula, used to place lime in the mouth. The majority of spatulas are made from wood and their designed handles display a variety of motifs, including a squatting human figure (see fig. 31), animals such as the lizard, snake and shark, plants and canoes. Rarer and more prestigious spatulas are made from bones of animals (such as the whale, the dugong and the cassowary) or humans, a particular type in the Trobriand and Marshall Bennett Islands being made from the bones of deceased relatives:

> Trobrianders have mixed feelings about the use of spatulas made from
> the bones of a husband or father. In the Trobriands the dead are buried
> twice. A day after the first burial the body is exhumed, the skull is
> made into a limepot and some of the bones into spatulas. The use of

31 Decorated lime spatulas from the Trobriand Islands. London, Museum of Mankind, Malinowski Collection.

the relics brings back pleasant memories of the deceased, but it is also regarded 'as a harsh and unpleasant duty, as a pious repayment for all the benefits received from the father'. The bones are used for some years, passed to more distant relations and finally deposited in caves.[5]

The mortars and pestles used to pulverise the areca nuts are less ornate on account of their more robust function. They are, nevertheless, decorated with animal and anthropomorphic motifs. Lime pots, as we have seen, have been made from human skulls, but the majority are made from coconuts or gourds. Woven fibres are used for their stoppers, and sometimes a boar's tusk is added for ornamental effect. In the Solomon Islands, to the east of the Massim cultural area, lime containers are made of bamboo (for an example incorporating Western influences see fig. 32). In the Massim cultures various kinds of baskets are used to carry betel-chewing equipment; among the Trobriand islanders the most prestigious is called *tanepopo*. This is actually a set of three nested baskets in which its high-ranking owner can hide some of his betel so that he will not be obliged to distribute his entire supply, as he would were all the nuts open to view. In some areas of Melanesia such

32 Lime container from the
Solomon Islands, decorated
with Western motifs. London,
Museum of Mankind.

traditional containers for the betel-chewing kit have been replaced by the practical, if rather prosaic, plastic carrier bag.

The cult of kava

> Long ago when the ancestors were alive, two women gathered wild yams and went to scrape their peels off in a tide pool at the sea. Mwatiktiki had brought to Tanna a kava plant and had hidden it in a hole in rocks on shore. The two women squatted down and began to scrape their yams. A kava shoot rose up and out, stuck in to the vagina of one of the women, and began to do it. She said to herself: 'I feel something good, something sweet!' The kava continued to do it. She turned to her sister and asked: 'what is poking me?' They saw that it was kava. They pulled out the kava shoot and carried it back to their garden at Isouragi where they planted it. At that time, men drank only wild kava. They had yet no knowledge of the real thing. The women did not tell anyone about the kava until it had grown large. They weeded it out in secret. They then dug it up, prepared food, and brought it to the kava-drinking ground and told men there that if they drank this kava, they would feel something different. Men quit drinking wild kava and began using kava. From that drinking ground, kava reached every area of the island. Women first discovered kava. Women weed kava and give it to men to drink. They bind it up and give it to men. Men had no kava. It was like that until our times. Now all us men have kava that women obtained.
>
> Lamont Lindstrom, *Drugs in Western Pacific Societies*

This tale of the origins of the domestication of kava was collected from Chiefs Nirua and Rapi by Lindstrom on the island of Tanna in Vanuatu (New Hebrides). As Lindstrom notes, this story contains a typical Melanesian theme in which women first discover items of cultural value only to lose them subsequently to men; historically the use of kava is indeed a male prerogative.

The species from which the kava beverage is made is *Piper methysticum* (a member of the pepper family), a shrub which grows up to a height of 4 metres (13 ft). In the traditional method of preparation, the roots and lower stems were chewed by children, uninitiated men or young female virgins. When the root had been chewed it was spat into a large bowl to which water

33 Kava cup from Fiji. London, Museum of Mankind.

was added; the infusion was then strained and poured into coconut cups (see fig. 33) from which it was subsequently drunk by adult men. A more recent method has been to grate or powder the root, thus eliminating the saliva content of the drink. Louis Lewin claimed to have been the first to investigate the pharmacological properties of kava, in the 1880s. In fact, he was preceded by the French pharmacists Cuzent and Gobley, who published their findings in the 1850s. Despite over a century of research, the analysis of the effects of kava is still, in some respects, incomplete. Emboden has suggested that in the traditional method of preparation by chewing, the alkaline saliva aids the extraction of the active ingredients marindin and dihydromethylsticin. Others have also claimed that the effects of kava differ depending on whether it is chewed or grated. Ron Brunton, who, like Lindstrom, has made a special field study of kava use in Vanuatu states:

> From my own experience I suspect that there is little, if any, difference
> in the effects of kava prepared by the alternative techniques. I have
> drunk kava prepared both by chewing and by grating on many
> separate occasions in Vanuatu, and with both I have experienced
> feelings of tranquillity, difficulty in maintaining motor co-ordinations,
> and eventual somnolence . . . in case it is countered that the only
> conclusion that can be drawn from my experiences with kava prepared

by different techniques is the importance of expectations and settings in structuring the subjective experience of drugs, two points should be noted. On the basis of what I had read, the first time I drank grated kava I fully expected that its effects would be *different* from the effects of chewed kava. Also, I drank grated kava only in bars or other westernised settings which were quite unlike those in which I drank chewed kava.[6]

Kava is found in the various parts of Melanesia (including New Guinea, New Britain, New Ireland, the Solomon Islands, Fiji and Vanuatu), throughout Polynesia (with the exception of Easter Island, New Zealand, the Chatham Islands and Rapa) and scarcely at all in Micronesia. In Melanesia kava drinking is practised only in certain regions, interspersed with groups of non-consumers, and Brunton considers that there are three possible explanations for this: (1) that there were never direct links between regions and that the psychoactive nature of kava was discovered independently in each area; (2) that there were direct trading links between regions, or a migration occurred: in either case the plant and / or knowledge of its preparation were transmitted; or (3) that such links were indirect and that the intermediary populations abandoned the use of the plant prior to European contact. On the basis of the botanical, linguistic, ethnological and rather scanty archaeological evidence, he concludes that the third explanation is almost certainly the right one.

So why was kava abandoned by various communities in Melanesia even before the arrival of European influences? As long ago as 1910 W.H.R. Rivers had sought to explain this by the movement into Melanesia of betel-using people who, in some areas, ousted the kava-using people. However, subsequent research has indicated that a more fruitful approach is to seek the explanation in the nature of the ritual authority of élites within the cultures in question. The historical record shows that, in the majority of cases, kava was consumed in ritual and religious contexts by élite male groups consisting of those who belonged to the upper grades of initiation and other cults (for a detailed account of certain Melanesian initiation cults and the restriction on the use of various intoxicants within them, see Chapter 5). Given that cultural instability and susceptibility to acculturation are well-known traits of many Melanesian societies, it should not surprise us to learn that rituals and the cults which organised them were often short-lived. In cases where kava consumption was an integral part of élite ceremonial life the loss of ritual power and authority often meant the abandonment of the drink itself. Yet in other areas of Melanesia the influence of Christianity and the subsequent secularisation and profanation of kava drinking brought problems of excessive use on the one hand and a religious reaction on the other, which in some cases resulted in individuals having revelations ordering its suppression in social and religious life. The French and British colonial authorities sought to ban the traditional method of chewing kava on the grounds that it was an unhygienic practice. This was probably a factor contributing both to the development of grated or powdered kava and the decline of kava rituals.

Traditional kava use, with its ceremonial restrictions, can be instructively compared with betel consumption. Betel was largely used in secular and informal contexts and its form allowed individuals to carry their own supply. The way in which kava was prepared made it impractical to carry on the person, and consumption was therefore largely limited to social gatherings and drinking in groups. Betel, as we have seen, was used by almost everyone and, in those societies which used it, any changes in the religious and social order were unlikely to eradicate its use in a single blow, whereas the survival of kava consumption was frequently reliant on that of the religious authority of an often small élite.

Tobacco and pituri in Aboriginal Australia

Although from a Western point of view tobacco has its origin in America, species of the *Nicotiana* genus have also been used as stimulants by indigenous populations in other parts of the world. The Australian Aborigines, for example, utilised a number of species, including *Nicotiana suaveolens* and *Nicotiana ingulba*. Donald Thomson, who led an expedition to the desert of central Western Australia in 1957, found that the Bindibu people of this arid region prepared a chewing quid from *Nicotiana ingulba*. It was made by first chewing the tobacco and then mixing in fine white ash from the burning of another plant (*Grevillea*). It is possible that the alkaloid ash served to quicken the effects of the nicotine. The chewing of this tobacco quid was not accompanied by ceremony or other formal behaviour but was used in a largely recreational fashion.

The situation in northern Australia was rather different. This area lacked a natural supply of tobacco and its peoples had to rely on supplies from Indonesian sailors and the inhabitants of the islands of the Torres Strait that divides Australia from New Guinea. The most regular trading was with the Torres islanders, who exchanged tobacco for Australian stone which they

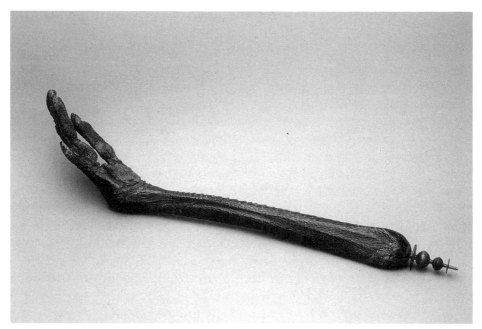

34 Australian pipe made from an emu's leg. London, Alfred Dunhill Collection.

needed as raw material for their axe industries. Despite this established trade route, shortages did occur and substitutes for tobacco were used. The Wik-mungkan used the leaves of a shrub which they called *yukk ponk mintjak* (*Grewia polygama*).

Although the northern populations must have known that tobacco could be chewed (through their interactions with seafarers), they preferred to smoke it. The consumption of tobacco was a highly ceremonial affair. Smoking naturally required the use of pipes and in the Northern Territories the passing around of a lit pipe became a ceremonial act, indicating the social solidarity of the participants. The pipes were made from a variety of materials. Those of the Cape York Peninsula (which show the influence of Papuan designs) were hollow wooden tubes, some of them made from bamboo that had drifted across the waters from eastern New Guinea and Eastern Indonesia. The pipes were called *marapi* and could be used simultaneously by two men. In Arnhem Land pipes were made from a remarkable array of natural objects, including crabs' claws, marine mollusc shells and even the humerus of certain birds such as the pelican and emu. Fig. 34 shows a pipe made from the leg of an emu, with modern bowl and mouthpiece added. The wooden pipes of Arnhem Land were cult objects and could only be smoked by fully initiated men. They were painted, carved or incised with sacred totemic signs and were often covered with a bark wrapping to keep them hidden from non-initiates (see fig. 35).

The Australian Aborigines also used an intoxicant called pituri (also written as pitcheri, pitchery, petgery and bedgery in early accounts). The identification of pituri has been the source of some confusion, as the term was used indiscriminately by some writers to refer to the tobacco used by the Aborigines before they came into contact with Westerners. Furthermore, the Aborigines who lived in areas devoid of traditional tobacco sources called the European tobacco 'white fella pituri', thus leading some to believe that pituri was tobacco, which it is not. Pituri is derived from *Duboisia hopwoodii*, a shrub growing 3–4 metres (10–13 ft) tall. It is found throughout the arid regions of all Australian states with the exception of Victoria and Tasmania. Even within this area it grows sparsely, and considerable effort was required on the part of the Aborigines to obtain sufficient amounts to satisfy their needs. Pituri was used to alleviate pain, hunger and fatigue. Among the active substances it contains is nicotine, which has, among other effects, that of increasing adrenalin flow and therefore stamina. Scopolamine is also found in pituri and causes excitement and hallucination; in larger doses it can be fatal. Indeed, the Aborigines used it in hunting the emu and

35 Totemic pipes from Arnhem Land, Australia. When in use, the design was covered in a sheathing of bark to keep it hidden from non-initiates. From Thompson 1939, fig. 6.

other game, poisoning water holes with the plant. According to Pamela Watson, the addictive qualities of pituri go far towards explaining its prominent role as an item of inter-tribal exchange.

The collection of branch tips and leaves usually took place in August, when the plant blossomed. It was the prerogative of the old men to select cuttings from the trees. The cuttings were placed in a specially dug and heated sand pit. The great secret of the correct preparation of pituri was the length of the steaming process. This knowledge was restricted literally to the greybeards (a man was considered a greybeard when grey first showed in his head hair or beard). After steaming, the pituri was taken from the pit and beaten with the edge of a boomerang to remove the larger twigs. The clean tips were then put into special pituri bags for transporting.

The intoxicant was normally consumed in the form of a quid, which was sometimes held together by the hair of the wallaby or the rabbit. Alkaline ash (usually from the *Acacia salicina*) was also added; this contributed to the chemical effects of the pituri in a similar way to the lime added to preparations of betel and coca. The quid was held between the lips or inside the cheek. On ceremonial occasions it was shared by being passed from mouth to mouth, the order of the chewers reflecting their rank in the social order, beginning with the most senior. An individual's quid was often stored behind the ear, which many European witnesses believed was done for convenience as the traditional near-nakedness of the Aborigines meant there was a lack of other places to keep it. In fact, in this position, the pituri continued to take effect transdermally (i.e. through the skin), as Watson explains: 'The area behind the ear is a particularly appropriate site for absorbing nicotine, being adjacent to a fine and extensive capillary system providing quick transport of the drug to the brain.'[7] In general, chewing pituri was preferred to smoking it, as it left both hands free for physical tasks. Smoking pituri became more common as tobacco use spread under European influence.

Large-scale expeditions were undertaken for the sole purpose of collecting pituri and were supervised by male elders. Such was the demand for it that the trade routes (known as pituri roads) covered vast distances across the outback. In contrast to most of the exchange systems practised by the Aborigines (which were based on transactions between trading partners bound by ties of mutual friendship), the exchange of pituri was often controlled by professional traders. Large markets with up to 500 participants took place along the major intersections of the pituri roads. The scarcity of the plant, the expert knowledge required to prepare it, and its habit-forming attributes made the exchange of pituri an activity which involved the wielding of economic and political power. Yet with the onslaught of white colonisation the expertise of the elders and the 'pituri clans' (which in some areas had a virtual monopoly on the collection, preparation, consumption and exchange of pituri) declined as traditional social structures underwent rapid change. The introduction of European tobacco was also a major factor in the decline of pituri use.

Despite the reported hallucinogenic and other psychoactive properties of pituri there is scant evidence that it played a role in the religious life of the Aborigines. There are, however, serious gaps in our knowledge of traditional Australian life and it is quite possible that the use of pituri in a religious context could have been missed by travellers and ethnographers alike, especially when one considers the secrecy surrounding the production and consumption of this particular intoxicant.

The rise of the smoking complex in the West

When Columbus landed on the north coast of Cuba on 5 November 1492 he was not only discovering a New World for Europe but also a highly addictive stimulant – tobacco. The scouts whom he sent inland returned with news of a strange custom indulged in by the inhabitants. Both men and women were reported to inhale the smoke of burning leaves rolled into a *tabaco*, or cigar. Jean Nicot de Villemain is generally credited with bringing the first tobacco to Europe when, in 1560, he brought *Nicotiana rustica* to the French court in the form of snuff (which, like the pipe and the cigar, was an American Indian innovation). He was in fact preceded by others, including an ex-Franciscan friar named André Thevet who had brought back tobacco seeds to France four years earlier. Being aware of the claims of his rivals, Nicot actively asserted his own case for having the new plant bear his name, and Linnaeus' subsequent naming of the tobacco genus *Nicotiana* crowned Nicot's undeserved success.

The earliest known instance of the use of tobacco in England was in 1556, when a Bristol sailor caused a sensation by smoking in the street. Sir John Hawkins was probably the first seafarer to import a consignment of tobacco into Britain when he arrived home in 1565 with *Nicotiana rustica* aboard, and in 1573 Sir Francis Drake intercepted a Spanish vessel in the Caribbean and returned to England with *Nicotiana tabacum* among the seized cargo. In the spring of 1585 Sir Walter Raleigh sent his cousin Sir Henry Grenville to Virginia in order to consolidate the new colony which had been named after the Virgin Queen, Elizabeth I. Among those who accompanied Grenville was Thomas Hariot, a mathematician and a good friend of Raleigh. Hariot wrote a lengthy report about Indian pipe smoking, in which he stated his belief that it expelled superfluous moisture from the body and opened all the pores, and that as a result the Indians were more healthy than the settlers. When Hariot and his companions returned home with Drake in 1586 they had become heavy smokers. In some popular accounts of the early days of tobacco use among Europeans the name of Raleigh is often invoked, but he was not directly involved in its introduction. He was, however, a serious smoker and did much to make the habit socially acceptable. A story, which seems to have been dreamed up by a later pipe smoker, relates that one night the Great Voyager introduced the Immortal Bard to the habit, but since there is no mention of it in any of Shakespeare's plays, it is unlikely that this tale has any basis in fact.

Although claims that Elizabeth I smoked are as tenuous as those concerning Shakespeare, she did tolerate the new habit. This tolerance was not, however, to continue, and when James I succeeded to the throne in 1603 he lost no time in expressing his views. In the very next year he published a short tract entitled *A Counterblaste to Tobacco*, in which he railed against the claims that it was a fine medicine and damned it as a filthy stinking habit. Rather accurately, as it turned out, he said it was harmful to the brain and dangerous to the lungs. Despite this royal condemnation the habit continued to gain adherents. Within a few years of tobacco entering the country the pro- and anti-smoking lobbies were thus already at loggerheads. The early seventeenth century saw the rapid expansion of the tobacco industry in the colonies of Virginia and Maryland. The London Company sent African slaves to Virginia to clear the forests and to plant and cultivate tobacco. It is estimated that as early as 1627 the Virginian plantations were producing as much as half a million pounds of tobacco per year.

Early English smokers used clay pipes based on American Indian originals. Owing to the high cost of tobacco, pipes were often shared and passed around in the *tabagies*, or smoking houses. The scarcity of tobacco was also reflected in the small size of the clays, which is why Elizabethan examples came to be known as elfin or fairy pipes. The tenacity of the Raleigh legend was further strengthened when a case of clays said to have belonged to him was obtained by the nineteenth-century pipe collector William Bragge. A Latin inscription on the case reads 'It has been my companion in this most unhappy time', a reference, presumably, to Raleigh's internment in the Tower of London. Despite this semblance of authenticity, this particular case, like others that have come on the market, is almost certainly a forgery.

Although tobacco consumption continued to rise in seventeenth-century Europe, taxation and overall cost (aggravated in England by the ban on domestic cultivation in favour of the Virginian colonists) prevented it from reaching the masses. It was particularly popular in ports and capital cities and among soldiers, who used it to keep hunger and cold at bay. New markets were constantly being opened and in 1697 Peter the Great, pushing aside the objections of the Orthodox Church, granted the East India Company a monopoly of the Russian market. In the eighteenth century tobacco was consumed in fashionable circles in the form of snuff, which was favoured partly because snuff taking uses less tobacco than smoking. The lavish and ornate snuff boxes of the period were clearly as much symbols of status as functional containers. Methods of snuff preparation and consumption also seem to have contributed to changes in fashions. The early eighteenth-century coats with large pockets (big enough to hold tobacco twists for making one's own snuff) were later replaced by tighter coats with smaller pockets into which a snuff box could easily fit once grinding one's own snuff had become *passé*.

Changes were also taking place in the world of pipe-making. A variety of materials were used to rival the clays: cherry, willow, gorse, oak and rosewood were popular choices for wooden pipes, and in both Britain (notably at the Staffordshire potteries) and on the Continent colourfully decorated porcelain pipes were being manufactured. In 1750 the discovery that a magnesium silicate (known as meerschaum or *écume de mer* on account of its likeness to petrified sea foam) could be used for pipe-making meant the days of the clay were numbered. Meerschaum was brought from Eskişehir in Turkey and Tanganyika (now Tanzania) and dominated the market until the most suitable material of all was found, by accident.

In the mid-nineteenth century a French pipe-maker on a pilgrimage to Napoleon's birthplace in Corsica lost (or broke) his meerschaum pipe. He employed a local peasant to make him a replacement out of wood, and so good was this new pipe that he sent a sample of the wood to St-Claude in France, where there was a specialist wood-turning factory. This town in a valley in the Jura mountains became the centre of the briar pipe industry and still maintains a prominent position in the world of quality pipe-making. The briar from which most modern pipes are made has no connection with the rose briar. The word derives from *bruyère*, the French name for *Erica arborea*, the white heath. British pipe manufacturers get their main supplies of the wood from France, Italy, Corsica and North America, although it

141

grows throughout the Mediterranean area. The arid climes in which it thrives make the root particularly tough and thus an ideal material for pipes. Experiments in cultivating the bush outside its natural habitat have been largely unsuccessful, as too much rainfall seems to limit its growth.

It is from the root (or burl) of the plant that pipes are made. Good-quality root is rare and often unobtainable. The best is considered to come from plants over forty-five years old, and some highly prized specimens have been growing for 250 years. A prime area for high-quality briar is the former Royal Forests of Rome. One of the problems facing the industry is that over-exploitation is not quickly remedied; young plants need considerable time in order to grow and reach sufficient quality. After locating suitable roots, sawyers cut them into pipe-sized blocks known as *ébauchons*. These are graded into four classes and then boiled in copper-lined vats for at least twelve hours in order to remove any living organisms. They are subsequently stacked in well-ventilated drying sheds, where the wood is left to season for about six months. During this seasoning period some of the *ébauchons* split and have to be thrown away, so that up to sixty roots may be required to yield the wood for a single top-quality pipe. The different grades of *ébauchon* are sacked up and exported in bales to pipe manufacturers all over the world. At auctions the manufacturers buy from landowners the right to take briar at a certain sum per 100 kilos for a period of years. There is an element of luck involved, as much apparently good wood, when opened and examined, is found to be flawed and therefore valueless. Recent attempts to limit this risk by X-raying the wood have not proved successful.

The manufacture of quality pipes in British factories involves some ninety-three processes, and only ten per cent of finished pipes reach the specifications required for a pipe of the highest grade; the rest are sold as lower-quality products. Machines are used to turn and shape the bowl and to turn and bore the stem, while the finer work of sanding, buffing, staining and polishing is all done by hand. Finally, a vulcanite mouthpiece is attached. Britain is famous for the fine pipes it produces, which are sought out by serious smokers all over the world. One rather unlikely owner was Josef Stalin, whom the British diplomat Sir Archibald Clark had seen struggling with an inferior Russian pipe during one of their meetings. On his next visit to Russia Clark brought Stalin six briars, a gift with which the Man of Steel was delighted. But the finer points of smoking were lost on him and he continued his preferred practice of crumbling up Russian cigarette tobacco and shoving it into the pipe.

Another statesman, Winston Churchill, was rarely seen without a large

Havana cigar. Like many other celebrities, he had a constant supply stored in the humidor room of an exclusive cigar importer, where they were kept at exactly the right temperature and level of humidity. The best cigars come from Cuba (the very best growing districts produce the famous Vuelto Abajo leaf) and Jamaica, but the leaf grown in India, Indonesia, the United States, Japan and South Africa is also good quality. A leading family of cigar producers fled from Castro's regime to set up business in the Canary Islands (which are close in latitude to Cuba), where they produce the best-selling cigar on the American market.

Now and increasingly cigarettes make up the bulk of world consumption of tobacco, even in countries such as Denmark and the Netherlands where cigar smoking is entrenched. The decline of cigarette smoking as a socially acceptable habit in the Western world has coincided with an increase of consumption in the developing world, where the habit is still growing.

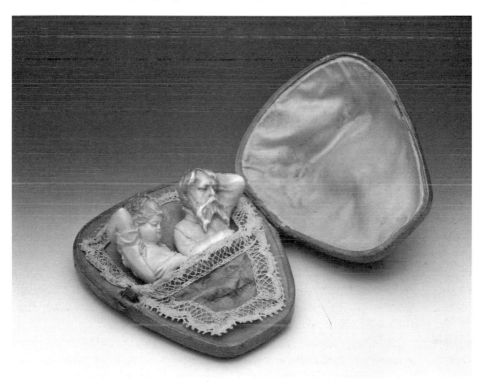

36 Two meerschaum cigar holders with amber mouthpieces. Carved in Vienna, *c.* 1875. London, Alfred Dunhill Collection.

Conclusion

· · · · · · ·

It remains to consider how the study of intoxicants in different societies can contribute towards an understanding of our own culture. Most communities have used psychoactive substances in both secular and sacred contexts; our own usage, which is almost exclusively secular, makes our culture in certain important respects the exception rather than the rule. Few societies pursue intoxication in the arbitrary and hedonistic fashion prevalent in the modern West. Our assimilation of stimulants such as tea and tobacco, first used in other cultures in sacred and ceremonial settings, has resulted in their being divested of any spiritual significance. Similarly, the development of synthetic derivatives such as heroin and cocaine from the exotic opium and coca has created a new era in intoxicant use. The highly addictive nature of such drugs often has devastating effects on regular users who, not having the economic means to sustain their habits within the law, turn to crime and thus create a major social problem. The use and abuse of intoxicants in our communities is part of a wider problem of secular society, namely that altered states of consciousness are not perceived as culturally valuable.

Great ingenuity and craftsmanship have been invested in creating the distinctive equipment that often accompanies the consumption of intoxicants. In traditional societies such artefacts reveal both the social status of the user and, in many cases, the sacred and symbolic importance of the altered states of consciousness with which they are associated. Items from our own culture such as cut-glass decanters, gold cigarette cases and porcelain tea sets reveal the economic standing of their owners and, at best, indicate good taste and aesthetic appreciation, but lack any spiritual value. Such embodiments of secularism, when introduced into traditional societies by way of trade, tend to erode the local ceremonial value of the intoxicants with which they are connected.

It is apparent that the legally sanctioned intoxicants of our present-day society are not given this status on account of any innate superiority they may have over other substances. The contemporary situation should rather be seen as an outgrowth of a long historical process with its roots stretching

144

back into prehistory. As I demonstrated in the opening chapter of this book, the use of opium and cannabis were important features of Neolithic social life long before the drinking complex spread throughout the continent. To our prehistoric forebears the introduction of alcoholic beverages was perhaps as shocking and socially unacceptable as the use of cannabis and opium is to many in our own society. Only a hundred years ago opium was readily available and legal, yet it is now seen as a dangerous narcotic. Changes in the status of tobacco have been even more rapid. Thirty years ago smoking was integral to adult social life and its popularity was epitomised in the media. Film stars could be seen smoking cigarette after cigarette – it was almost anti-social not to smoke! Yet today in public places such as restaurants it is the smoker who has to seek out that small area permitted for his or her habit, and the main area, once the smoker's domain, is now the social space of the non-smoker. Smoking seems to be a habit destined for a slow but inevitable decline in Western culture.

The introduction of tobacco smoking into Europe, described in Chapter 7, was spearheaded by sailors, entrepreneurs and other travellers who picked up the exotic habit and brought it home with them. Similarly, troops returning from the Napoleonic wars brought cannabis back to France. Such individuals and social groups have played a significant role in the trans-mission of various intoxicants throughout the world, as numerous other examples in this book have demonstrated. Seekers after scientific or poetic truth have also been among the first to experiment with new or little-known psychoactive substances and have likewise acted as catalysts for social change. Among the significant scientific contributions have been the dis-covery by ethnobotanists of numerous intoxicating species and the isolation of their psychoactive principles by pharmacologists and biochemists. Poets and other imaginative writers, with their special aptitude for describing the subtle nature of subjective experience, have added an essential dimension to our understanding of altered states of consciousness induced by intoxi-cants. The psychological study of the 'cartography of inner space', as Roland Fischer calls it, represents an approach through the middle ground between natural science and art in its mapping of the meditative and hallucinogenic states in relation to the ordinary state of waking consciousness.

One of the distinctive features of the anthropological approach is its emphasis on describing the socio-cultural frameworks in which individual experiences of intoxication take place. Societies tend not only to distinguish normal from altered states of consciousness but also between legitimate and illicit types of the latter. Some states of intoxication are seen as valid ways

145

of pursuing spiritual goals – or simply as pleasurable experiences – whilst others are considered essentially negative and harmful to both the individual and society as a whole. Elites, whether they are Western politicians or tribal shamans, seek to influence members of their communities by restricting access to both legitimate intoxicants (often the privilege of a chosen few) and illicit substances. In many societies, including our own, there is a struggle between factions over which intoxicants are acceptable. That is to say, there is a political, and sometimes spiritual, conflict over the nature of consciousness itself. Since societies are not isolated from one another, but in a continuous state of interaction, this struggle takes place not only within communities but also between them.

By studying the use of intoxicants in societies radically different from our own, anthropology can counteract the tendency to perceive our own practices and values as universal models for human behaviour. I have shown that in some important respects our own culture's relationship with intoxicants is an unusual one and that to use it as a gauge by which to measure others is misleading. Reductionists in our society – and in anthropology itself – seek to deny any 'reality' to altered states of consciousness induced by psychoactive substances, treating them as illusions and distorted reflections of everyday consciousness. I do not deny that the inner worlds described by informants are more or less chimerical versions of a society's natural and cultural milieu, yet it is nevertheless an error to reduce these inner worlds to passive projections of the external order of things. Many of the ethnographic accounts given in this book bear witness to the active role which altered states of consciousness play in the shaping of culture.

In recent years the West has begun to appreciate the fact that tribal societies can teach us much about the natural world from which we are so often alienated. It seems we may also have much to learn about the supernatural world, from which we are likewise alienated. Bearing in mind that humans have an innate need to experience altered states of consciousness, to ignore or repress our own natures in this way is to neglect our own capacities. What anthropology can do, by describing other cultures in which scientific and poetic approaches to truth are part of a holistic vision, is to remind us of the lack of harmony in the elements of our own second nature. It can indicate ways in which we may reach a better understanding of the importance of altered states of consciousness in both our collective and our personal lives.

Notes

· · · · · · ·

Introduction

1. In terms of its psychoactive effects kava is best classified as a hypnotic, but its cultural role is comparable to that of stimulants, and it is therefore discussed in Chapter 7.
2. The transliteration of indigenous botanical terms and other foreign words has, as a rule, been simplified throughout this work.

Chapter One   **Stone Age Alchemy**

1. Sahlins 1972, 34.
2. Ibid., 35.
3. Binford and Binford, quoted in Feyerabend 1982, 104.
4. Leroi-Gourhan 1982, 13.
5. Lévi-Strauss 1966, 3.
6. Wasson 1971, 208.
7. Lewis-Williams and Dowson 1988, 202.
8. Sherratt 1991, 54.
9. Merrillees 1962, 288.
10. Ibid., 292.
11. As Emboden points out, the word hemp is sometimes used in a loose, general way as a term referring to a variety of plant fibres. My use of the term refers solely to the fibres derived from the *Cannabis sativa* species.
12. Herodotus IV, 74.
13. Emboden, in Furst (ed.) 1972, 223.
14. Sherratt 1987, 91.
15. Ibid., 89.

Chapter Two   **Frozen Tombs and Fly-Agaric Men**

1. See Kent 1950, inscriptions XPh 26, DSe 24–5, DNa 25.
2. Herodotus IV, 75.
3. See Dunn 1973, 488–9, note 2, for additional details concerning these petroglyphs.
4. Jochelson 1908, 583.
5. Dunn 1973, 490–1.

Chapter Three   **The Mystery of *Haoma***

1. Emboden 1979, 59.

2. The latter half of mandala X, a later addition to the *Rig Veda*, is an exception, but this in itself does not affect the validity of Wasson's argument.
3. Wasson 1971, 23.
4. Humbach 1991, vol I, 178.
5. Flattery and Schwartz 1989, 105.
6. Ibid., 6, note 4.
7. Parry 1982, 105, note 31.
8. Bourke 1891, 335 and 337.
9. Windfuhr 1985, 723.
10. Wasson 1971, 157 and 178.
11. Haug and West 1872, 165.
12. Ibid., 174.

Chapter Four **American Dreams**

1. Emboden 1979, 102.
2. In Furst (ed.) 1972, 100.
3. Collection no. 1169.
4. In Dobkin de Rios 1974, 156.
5. Schleiffer 1973, 19–20.
6. Leonard 1942, 326.
7. Duerr 1985, 154.
8. Radin 1957, 404.
9. Ibid., 407.
10. King 1977, 12.

Chapter Five **The Alchemists of Afek**

1. Emboden 1979, 70–1.
2. Afek means 'old woman' in a number of Mountain Ok languages, and it is as a woman that 'she' appears in the various myths of the region. However, that Afek is said to have semen shows that 'she' is seen as a being with androgynous attributes. It is interesting to note that in the Western alchemical tradition the androgynous being is a common motif representing the spiritually perfect human. There is an analogy here with the senior elders of the twelfth degree of the Bimin-Kuskusmin hierarchy, who identify themselves with Afek during the taking of the highest sacred substance.
3. Poole in Lindstrom (ed.) 1987, 185.
4. Barth 1987, 73.

Chapter Six **Lucifer's Garden**

1. Witches and sorcerers also administered killing ointments by rubbing poisons into the bodies of their sleeping victims.
2. Quoted in Harner 1973, 130–1.
3. Harner 1973, 131.
4. Emboden 1979, 126.

Notes

5. Schenk 1956, 29.
6. Schenk in Harner (ed.) 1973, 139–40.
7. Wasson 1971, 189.
8. Polo 1959, 48.
9. Emboden in Furst (ed.) 1972, 228.
10. Baudelaire 1986, 122.
11. Ibid., 108.
12. See Symonds and Grant 1971, 843, note 4.
13. Leary 1970, 19.
14. Burroughs and Ginsberg 1963, 12.
15. Brady 1992, 2.
16. Bourgois 1989, 9.

Chapter Seven   **Stimulating Society**

1. Weir 1985, 41–2.
2. Baker 1972, 110–11.
3. Brownrigg 1991, 11.
4. Gell 1975, 124.
5. Beran 1988, 51.
6. Brunton 1989, 5–6.
7. Watson 1983, 27.

Bibliography
· · · · · · · ·

Aiston, G., 1937. 'The Aboriginal narcotic pitcheri', *Oceania* VII (1936–7), 372–7.

Apuleius, 1988. *The Golden Ass*, trans. Robert Graves, Penguin Books, Harmondsworth.

Avesta: see Humbach 1991.

Babor, T., 1988. *Alcohol: Customs and Rituals*, Encyclopedia of Psychoactive Drugs, Burke Publishing Company Ltd, London.

Bahn, P.G. and J. Vertut, 1988. *Images of the Ice Age*, Windward, Leicester, and Facts on File, New York.

Baker, H.G., 1972. *Plants and Civilization*, 2nd edn, Macmillan Press Ltd, London and Basingstoke.

Barth, F., 1975. *Ritual and Knowledge among the Baktaman of New Guinea*, Universitetsforlaget, Oslo, and Yale University Press, New Haven.

Barth, F., 1987. *Cosmologies in the Making: A Generative Approach to Cultural Variation in Inner New Guinea*, Cambridge University Press, Cambridge.

Barth, F., 1989. 'The analysis of culture in complex societies', *Ethnos* 54, 120–42.

Barth, F., 1991. 'The guru and the conjurer: transactions in knowledge and the shaping of culture in Southeast Asia and Melanesia', *Man* (n.s.) 25, 640–53.

Baudelaire, C., 1986. 'The Poem of Hashish', in *My Heart Laid Bare and Other Prose Writings*, trans. N. Cameron, Soho Book Company, London.

Beran, H., 1988. *Betel-chewing Equipment of East New Guinea*, Shire Ethnography no. 8, Shire Publications Ltd, Aylesbury.

Blagg, T., 1978. *The Nomads of Eastern Siberia*, British Museum Publications, London.

Blofeld, J., 1985. *The Chinese Art of Tea*, George Allen and Unwin, London.

Bogoras, W., 1904. *The Chukchee*, The Jesup North Pacific Expedition, Memoir of the American Museum of Natural History, vol. VII, E.J. Brill, Leiden, and G.E. Stechert, New York.

Bourgois, P., 1989. 'Crack in Spanish Harlem: culture and economy in the inner city', *Anthropology Today*, vol. 5, no. 4, 6–11.

Bourke, J.G., 1891. *Scatologic Rites of All Nations*, W.H. Lowdermilk & Co., Washington, DC.

Boyce, M., 1970. 'Haoma, priest of the sacrifice', in M. Boyce and I. Gershevitch (eds), *W.B. Henning Memorial Volume*, Asia Major Library, Lund Humphries, London.

Boyce, M., 1975. *A History of Zoroastrianism*, vol. I, E.J. Brill, Leiden and Cologne.

Boyce, M., 1977. *A Persian Stronghold of Zoroastrianism*, based on the Ratanbai Katrak lectures 1975, Clarendon Press, Oxford.

Boyce, S.S., 1900. *Hemp (Cannabis sativa)*, Orange Judd Company, New York.

Bibliography

Bradley, R., 1989. 'Deaths and entrances: a contextual analysis of megalithic art', *Current Anthropology* 30/1, 68–75.

Brady, M., 1992. *Heavy Metal: The Social Meaning of Petrol Sniffing in Australia*, Aboriginal Studies Press, Canberra.

Bragge, W., 1880. *Bibliotheca Nicotiana*, privately published, Birmingham.

Brody, H., 1971. *Indians on Skid Row*, Northern Science Research Group, Department of Indian Affairs and Northern Development, Ottawa.

Brough, J., 1971. 'Soma and *Amanita muscaria*', *Bulletin of the School of Oriental and African Studies* XXXIV, part 2, 331–62.

Brough, J., 1973. 'Problems of the "soma-mushroom" theory', *Indologica Taurinensia* I, 21–32.

Brownrigg, H., 1991. *Betel Cutters from the Samuel Eilenberg Collection*, Edition Hansjörg Mayer, Stuttgart and London.

Brunton, R., 1989. *The Abandoned Narcotic: Kava and Cultural Instability in Melanesia*, Cambridge University Press, Cambridge.

Burroughs, W.S. and A. Ginsberg, 1963. *The Yage Letters*, City Lights Books, San Francisco.

Burton, R.F., 1851. *Sindh, and the Races that Inhabit the Valley of the Indus*, W.H. Allen & Co., London.

Burton-Bradley, B.G., 1972. 'Betel chewing', in P. Ryan (ed.), *Encyclopedia of Papua and New Guinea*, vol. 1, 66–7, Melbourne University Press, Carlton, Victoria.

Caro Baroja, J., 1964. *The World of the Witches*, trans. N. Glendinning, Weidenfeld and Nicolson, London.

Cassanelli, L., 1986. 'Qat: changes in the production and consumption of a quasilegal commodity in northeast Africa', in A. Appadurai (ed.), *The Social Life of Things: Commodities in Cultural Perspective*, Cambridge University Press, Cambridge.

Chagnon, N.A., P. Le Quesne and J.M. Cook, 1971. 'Yanomamö hallucinogens: anthropological, botanical and chemical findings', *Current Anthropology*, vol. 12, no. 1, 72–4.

Clark, A.J., 1921. 'Flying ointments', in M.A. Murray, *The Witch-Cult in Western Europe: A Study in Anthropology*, Appendix V, 279–80, Clarendon Press, Oxford.

Cooke, M.C., 1860. *The Seven Sisters of Sleep: Popular History of the Seven Prevailing Narcotics of the World*, James Blackwood, London.

Cooke, M.C., 1871. *Handbook of British Fungi*, 2 vols, Macmillan & Co., London.

Corti, E., 1931. *A History of Smoking*, trans. P. England, George Harrap & Co. Ltd, London.

Crowley, A., 1909–13. *The Equinox: The Official Organ of the A. A.* London (various publishers).

Crowley, A., 1917. 'Cocaine', *The International* (October), 291–4, New York.

Crowley, A., 1955. *777 Revised*, The Neptune Press, London.

Dobkin de Rios, M., 1973. 'Curing with *Ayahuasca* in an urban slum', in Harner (ed.) 1973.

Dobkin de Rios, M., 1974. 'The influence of psychotropic flora and fauna on Maya religion', *Current Anthropology*, vol. 15, no. 2, 147–64.

Douglas, M. (ed.), 1991. *Constructive Drinking: Perspectives on Drink from Anthropology*, Cambridge University Press, Cambridge.

Bibliography

Du Toit, B.M. (ed.), 1977. *Drugs, Rituals and Altered States of Consciousness*, A.A. Balkema, Rotterdam.

Duerr, H.P., 1985. *Dreamtime: Concerning the Boundary between Wildness and Civilization*, Basil Blackwell, Oxford.

Dunhill, A., 1977. *The Pipe Book*, rev. edn, Arthur Barker Ltd, London.

Dunhill, A.H., 1976. *The Gentle Art of Smoking*, Max Reinhardt, London.

Dunn, E., 1973. 'Russian use of *Amanita muscaria*: a footnote to Wasson's *Soma*', *Current Anthropology*, vol. 14, no. 4, 488–92.

Efron, D.H., B. Holmstedt and N.S. Kline (eds), 1979. *Ethnopharmacological Search for Psychoactive Drugs*, Raven Press, New York.

Eliade, M., 1969. *Yoga, Immortality and Freedom*, trans. W.R. Trask, Bollingen Series LVI, Princeton University Press, Princeton.

Eliade, M., 1972. *Shamanism: Archaic Techniques of Ecstasy*, Bollingen Foundation, Princeton University Press, Princeton.

Emboden, W., 1974. *Bizarre Plants: Magical, Monstrous, Mythical*. Studio Vista, London.

Emboden, W., 1979. *Narcotic Plants: Hallucinogens, Stimulants, Inebriants, and Hypnotics, their Origins and Uses*, Studio Vista, London.

Evans, J., 1989. 'Report' concerning Robert S. Merrilees' *Highs and Lows in the Holy Land: Opium in Biblical Times*, in *Eretz-Israel*, vol. 20, Yigael Yadin Memorial Volume, 153–4, Israel Exploration Society, Jerusalem.

Evans-Pritchard, E.E., 1962. *Essays in Social Anthropology*. Faber and Faber, London.

Fagg, W., 1976. 'Correspondence: the sacred mushroom in Scandinavia', *Man* (n.s.) 2, 440.

Feyerabend, P., 1982. *Science in a Free Society*, Verso Editions/New Left Books, London.

Feyerabend, P, 1988. *Against Method*, rev. edn, Verso, London and New York.

Fischer, R., 1975. 'Cartography of inner space', in R.K. Siegel and L.J. West (eds), *Hallucinations: Behaviour, Experience and Theory*, John Wiley and Sons, New York and London.

Flattery, D.S. and M. Schwartz, 1989. *Haoma and Harmaline: The Botanical Identity of the Indo-Iranian Sacred Hallucinogen 'Soma' and its Legacy in Religion, Language, and Middle Eastern Folklore*, University of California Press, Berkeley, Los Angeles and London.

Frazer, J.G., 1987. *The Golden Bough: A Study in Magic and Religion*, abridged edn, Papermac, Macmillan Publishers Ltd, London.

Furst, P.T. (ed.), 1972. *Flesh of the Gods: The Ritual Use of Hallucinogens*, George Allen and Unwin Ltd, London.

Furst, P.T., 1988. *Mushrooms*, Encyclopedia of Psychoactive Drugs, 2nd edn, Burke Publishing Company Ltd, London.

Gardiner-Garden, J.R., 1978a. *Ktesias on Early Central Asian History and Ethnography*, Papers on Inner Asia, no. 6, Bloomington, Indiana.

Gardiner-Garden, J.R., 1978b. *Herodotos' Contemporaries on Skythian Geography and Ethnography*, Papers on Inner Asia, no. 10, Bloomington, Indiana.

Gell, A., 1975. *Metamorphosis of the Cassowaries: Umeda Society, Language and Ritual*, LSE Mono-

Bibliography

graphs on Social Anthropology, no. 51. The Athlone Press, London.

Gershevitch, I., 1974. 'An Iranianist's view of the soma controversy', in P. Gignoux and A. Tafazzoli (eds), *Mémorial Jean de Menasce*, Imprimerie Orientaliste, Louvain, and Fondation Culturelle Iranienne, Tehran.

Glowa, J.R., 1988. *Inhalants: The Toxic Fumes*, Encyclopedia of Psychoactive Drugs, Burke Publishing Company Ltd, London.

Goodman, F.D., J.H. Henney and E. Pressel, 1974. *Trance, Healing and Hallucination: Three Field Studies in Religious Experience*, John Wiley and Sons, New York and London.

Grzimek, B. (ed.), 1974. *Grzimek's Animal Life Encyclopedia*, vol. 5, Van Nostrand Reinhold Company, New York and London.

Haining, P. (ed.), 1975. *The Hashish Club: An Anthology of Drug Literature*, 2 vols, Peter Owen, London.

Halifax, J., 1982. *Shaman: The Wounded Healer*, Thames and Hudson, London.

Harner, M.J., 1973. 'The role of hallucinogenic plants in European witchcraft', in Harner (ed.) 1973.

Harner, M.J. (ed.), 1973. *Hallucinogens and Shamanism*, Oxford University Press, London, Oxford and New York.

Harrington, J.P., 1932. *Tobacco among the Karuk Indians of California*, Bulletin 94, Smithsonian Institution, Bureau of American Ethnology, Washington, DC.

Hartman, S.S., 1980. *Parsism: The Religion of Zoroaster*, Iconography of Religions XIV, 4, Institute of Religious Iconography, State University, Groningen, and E.J. Brill, Leiden.

Haug, M and E.W. West, 1872. *The Book of Arda Viraf*, Trubner & Co., London.

Hayter, A., 1968. *Opium and the Romantic Imagination*, Faber and Faber, London.

Heath, E.G. and V. Chiara, 1977. *Brazilian Indian Archery: A Preliminary Ethno-Toxological Study of the Archery of the Brazilian Indians*, The Simon Archery Foundation, Manchester Museum, Manchester.

Herodotus, 1880. *Histories*, trans. G. Rawlinson, John Murray, London.

Hill, B.W.S., 1978. 'Studies on *Erica arborea* with reference to the briar pipe industry', unpublished PhD thesis, University of Bath.

Humbach, H., 1991. *The Gathas of Zarathustra and the Other Old Avestan Texts*, 2 vols, Carl Winter, Universitätsverlag, Heidelberg.

Jettmar, K. (ed.), 1974. *Cultures of the Hindukush: Selected Papers from the Hindu Kush Cultural Conference Held at Moesgård 1970*, Franz Steiner Verlag, Wiesbaden.

Jettmar, K., 1986. *The Religions of the Hindukush, vol. I, The Religion of the Kafirs: The Pre-Islamic Heritage of Afghan Nuristan*, trans. A. Nayyar, Aris and Phillips, Warminster.

Jochelson, W., 1908. *The Koryak*, The Jesup North Pacific Expedition, Memoir of the American Museum of Natural History, vol. VI, E.J. Brill, Leiden, and G.E. Stechert, New York.

Junger, E., 1969. 'Drugs and ecstasy', in J.M. Kitagawa and C.H. Long (eds), *Myths and Symbols, Studies in Honor of Mircea Eliade*, University of Chicago Press, Chicago and London.

Kaplan, R.W., 1975. 'The sacred mushroom in Scandinavia', *Man* (n.s.) 10, 72–9.

Kent, R.G., 1950. *Old Persian: Grammar, Texts, Lexicon*, American Oriental Society, New Haven.

Bibliography

King, J.C.H., 1977. *Smoking Pipes of the North American Indians*, British Museum Publications, London.

La Barre, W., 1970. Review of R. Gordon Wasson, *Soma: Divine Mushroom of Immortality*, *American Anthropologist*, vol. 72, no. 2, 368–73.

Lamantia, P., 1959. *Narcotica*, The Auerhahn Press, San Francisco.

Leary, T., 1970. *The Politics of Ecstasy*, MacGibbon and Kee, London.

Leonard, I.A., 1942. 'Peyote and the Mexican Inquisition, 1620', *American Anthropologist* (n.s.), vol. 44, no. 2, 324–6.

Leroi-Gourhan, A., 1982. *The Dawn of European Art: An Introduction to Palaeolithic Cave Painting*. Cambridge University Press, Cambridge.

Lévi-Strauss, C., 1966. *The Savage Mind*, Weidenfeld and Nicolson, London.

Lévi-Strauss, C., 1977. 'Mushrooms in culture: apropos of a book by R.G. Wasson', in *Structural Anthropology*, vol. II, trans. M. Layton, Allen Lane, London.

Levin, M.G. and L.P. Potapov (eds), 1964. *The Peoples of Siberia*, University of Chicago Press, Chicago and London.

Lewin, L., 1964. *Phantastica: Narcotic and Stimulating Drugs, Their Use and Abuse*, Routledge and Kegan Paul, London.

Lewis, B., 1967. *The Assassins: A Radical Sect in Islam*, Weidenfeld and Nicolson, London.

Lewis-Williams, J.D., 1991a. 'Wrestling with analogy: a methodological dilemma in Upper Palaeolithic art research', *Proceedings of the Prehistoric Society* 57, part I, 149–62.

Lewis-Williams, J.D., 1991b. 'Upper Palaeolithic art in the 1990s: a southern African perspective', *South African Journal of Science* 87, September 1991, 422–9.

Lewis-Williams, J.D. and T.A. Dowson, 1988. 'The signs of all times: entoptic phenomena in Upper Palaeolithic art', *Current Anthropology* 29/2, 201–45.

Lewis-Williams, J.D. and T.A. Dowson, 1993. 'On vision and power in the Neolithic: evidence from the decorated monuments', *Current Anthropology* 34/1, 55-65.

Lindstrom, L., 1987. 'Drunkenness and gender on Tanna, Vanuatu', in Lindstrom (ed.) 1987.

Lindstrom, L. (ed.) 1987. *Drugs in Western Pacific Societies: Relations of Substance*, ASAO Monograph no. 11, University Press of America, Lanham, New York and London.

Lovejoy, P.E., 1980. *Caravans of Kola: The Hausa Kola Trade 1700–1900*. Ahmadu Bello University Press Ltd, Zaria, Nigeria.

Marshack, A., 1991. *The Roots of Civilization: The Cognitive Beginnings of Man's First Art, Symbol, and Notation*, 2nd edn, Moyer Bell, Mount Kisco.

Merlin, M.D., 1984. *On the Trail of the Ancient Opium Poppy*, Associated University Presses, London and Toronto.

Merrillees, R.S., 1962. 'Opium trade in the Bronze Age Levant', Antiquity XXXVI, 287–92.

Mithen, S., 1988. 'Looking and learning: Upper Palaeolithic art and information gathering', *World Archaeology* 19/3, 297–327.

Morgan, A., 1987. 'Who put the toad in toadstool?' *New Scientist*, 25 December 1986/1 January 1987, 44–7.

Bibliography

Morgan, T., 1988. *Literary Outlaw: The Life and Times of William S. Burroughs*, Henry Holt & Co., New York (published in the UK by Pimlico, 1991).

Murray, M.A., 1952. *The God of the Witches*, Faber and Faber, London.

Needham, J., 1970. *Clerks and Craftsmen in China and the West*, Cambridge University Press, Cambridge.

Needham, R., 1978, *Primordial Characters*. University Press of Virginia, Charlottesville.

O'Flaherty, W.D., 1981. *The Rig Veda: An Anthology*, Penguin Books, Harmondsworth.

Parry, J., 1982. 'Sacrificial death and the necrophagous ascetic', in M. Bloch and J. Parry (eds), *Death and the Regeneration of Life*, Cambridge University Press, Cambridge.

Pliny, 1969. *Natural History*, vol. VI, books XX–XXIII, trans. W.H.S. Jones, Loeb Classical Library, Harvard University Press, Cambridge, Massachusetts, and William Heinemann, London.

Polo, Marco, 1959. *The Travels*, André Deutsch, London.

Polsky, N., 1971. *Hustlers, Beats and Others*, Penguin Books, Harmondsworth.

Poole, F.J.P., 1987. 'Ritual rank, the self, and ancestral power: liturgy and substance in a Papua New Guinea society', in Lindstrom (ed.) 1987.

Pritchett, R.T., 1890. *Ye Smokiana*, privately published, London.

Radin, P., 1957. *Primitive Man as Philosopher*, Dover Books, New York.

Ratsch, C. (ed.), 1989. *Gateway to Inner Space: A Festschrift in Honor of Albert Hofmann*, trans. J. Baker, Prism Press, Bridport, Dorset.

Reay, M., 1960. ' "Mushroom madness" in the New Guinea Highlands', Oceania XXXI, 137–9.

Reichel-Dolmatoff, G., 1972. 'The cultural context of an Aboriginal hallucinogen: *Banisteriopsis caapi*', in Furst (ed.) 1972.

Reichel-Dolmatoff, G., 1987. *Shamanism and Art of the Eastern Tukanoan Indians*, E.J. Brill, Leiden.

Renfrew, J.M., 1973. *Palaeoethnobotany: The Prehistoric Food Plants of the Near East and Europe*, Methuen & Co., London.

Riedlinger, T.J. (ed.), 1990. *The Sacred Mushroom Seeker: Essays for R. Gordon Wasson*, Ethnomycological Studies, no. 11, Dioscorides Press, Portland, Oregon.

Rig Veda: see O'Flaherty 1981.

Roaf, M., 1974. 'The subject peoples on the base of the statue of Darius', *Cahiers Dafi* IV, 73–160.

Robbins, R.H., 1959. *The Encyclopedia of Witchcraft and Demonology*, Peter Nevill, London.

Rolle, R., 1989. *The World of the Scythians*, trans. G. Walls, Batsford, London.

Rudenko, S.I., 1970. *Frozen Tombs of Siberia: The Pazyryk Burials of Iron-Age Horsemen*, trans. M.W. Thompson, Dent, London.

Sahlins, M., 1972. *Stone Age Economics*, Tavistock Publications Ltd, London.

Schenk, G., 1956. *The Book of Poisons*, trans. M. Bullock, Weidenfeld and Nicolson, London.

Schleiffer, H., 1973. *Sacred Narcotic Plants of the New World Indians: An Anthology of Texts from the Sixteenth Century to Date*, Hafner Press, New York.

Schlotterbeck, J.O., F.E. Stewart and J.V. Shoemaker, 1894. *An Illustrated Monograph on Kola*, Frederick Stearns & Co., Detroit.

Bibliography

Schmidt, E.F., 1953, 1957, 1970. *Persepolis*, vol. I *Structures, Reliefs, Inscriptions* (1953); vol. II *Contents of the Treasury and Other Discoveries* (1957); vol. III *The Royal Tombs and Other Monuments* (1970), University of Chicago Press, Chicago.

Schultes, R.E., 1972. 'An overview of hallucinogens in the western hemisphere', in Furst (ed.) 1972.

Schultes, R. E. and A. Hofmann, 1980. *Plants of the Gods: Origins of Hallucinogenic Use*, Hutchinson & Co., London.

Seligmann, K., 1948. *The History of Magic*, Pantheon Books, New York.

Sherratt, A.G., 1987. 'Cups that cheered', in W.H. Waldren and R.C. Kennard (eds), *Bell-Beakers of the West Mediterranean*, British Archaeological Reports, International Series 331, Oxford.

Sherratt, A.G., 1991. 'Sacred and profane substances: the ritual use of narcotics in later Neolithic Europe', in P. Garwood, D. Jennings, R. Skeates and J. Toms (eds), *Sacred and Profane: Proceedings of a Conference on Archaeology, Ritual and Religion*, Oxford University Committee for Archaeology, Monograph no. 32, Oxford.

Siegel, R.K., 1989. *Intoxication: Life in Pursuit of Artificial Paradise*, Simon and Schuster, London and New York.

Siegel, R.K. and M.E. Jarvik, 1975. 'Drug-induced hallucinations in animals and man', in R.K. Siegel and L.J. West (eds), *Hallucinations: Behaviour, Experience, and Theory*, John Wiley and Sons, New York and London.

Spedding, A.L., 1989. 'Coca eradication: a remedy for independence?' with a postscript, *Anthropology Today*, vol. 5, no. 5, 4–9.

Strathern, M., 1987. 'Relations without substance', in Lindstrom (ed.) 1987.

Sundström, L., 1966. 'The cola nut: functions in West African social life', *Varia* II, Studia Ethnographica Uppsaliensia XXVI, 135–49.

Svatmarama, 1972. *The Hathayogapradipika*, Adyar Library and Research Centre, Madras.

Symonds, J., 1973. *The Great Beast*, rev. edn, Mayflower Books, Frogmore, St Albans.

Symonds, J. and K. Grant (eds), 1971. *'The Confessions of Aleister Crowley*, Bantam Books, Toronto, New York and London.

Thompson, C.J.S., 1934. *The Mystic Mandrake*, Rider & Co., London.

Thomson, D.F., 1939. 'Notes on the smoking pipes of North Queensland and the Northern Territory of Australia', *Man* XXXIX (June), 81–91.

Thomson, D.F., 1961. 'A narcotic from *Nicotiana ingulba*, used by the Desert Bindibu: chewing of a true tobacco in Central Australia', *Man* LXI (January), 5–8.

Torres, C.M., 1987. *The Iconography of South American Snuff Trays and Related Paraphernalia*. Ethnologiska Studier 37, Göteborg.

Ucko, P.J. and A. Rosenfeld, 1967. *Palaeolithic Cave Art*, Weidenfeld and Nicolson, London.

Usdin, E. and D.H. Efron, 1979. *Psychotropic Drugs and Related Compounds*, 2nd edn, Pergamon Press, Oxford and New York.

Wasson, R.G., 1971. *Soma: Divine Mushroom of Immortality*. Ethno-mycological Studies, no. 1, Harcourt Brace Jovanovich Inc., New York.

Bibliography

Wasson, R.G., 1972. *Soma and the Fly-Agaric: Mr Wasson's Rejoinder to Professor Brough*, Botanical Museum of Harvard University Ethno-mycological Studies, no. 2, Cambridge, Massachusetts.

Watson, P., 1983. *This Precious Foliage: A Study of the Aboriginal Psycho-active Drug Pituri*, University of Sydney, Sydney.

Weil, G.M., R. Metzner and T. Leary (eds), 1965. *The Psychedelic Reader, Selected from the Psychedelic Review*, University Books, New York.

Weir, S., 1985. *Qat in Yemen: Consumption and Social Change*, British Museum Publications, London.

Windfuhr, G.L., 1985. 'Haoma/soma: the plant', in *Papers in Honour of Professor Mary Boyce*, Acta Iranica 25, E.J. Brill, Leiden.

Zaehner, R.C., 1957. *Mysticism Sacred and Profane*, Clarendon Press, Oxford.

Zaehner, R.C., 1972. *Drugs, Mysticism and Make-Believe*, Collins, London.

Illustration Acknowledgements

The author and publishers would like to thank all those institutions and individuals who have kindly supplied illustrations or given permission to reproduce works which are their copyright. In addition to the acknowledgements given in the captions, the drawings in figs 3 (after J. Green, *Megalithic Monuments of the Morbihan*, Pitkin Pictorials, London 1984), 5 and 18 are by Susan Bird. Fig. 1 is from the Mary Evans Picture Library; figs 9 and 11 are from the Harry Smith Horticultural Photographic Collection; fig. 19 is by Chris Mattison (*Frogs and Toads of the World*, Blandford, London 1992), and fig. 29 is courtesy of the International Coffee Organisation.

Index

Aborigines, Australian 109–11, 135–9
Acacia salicina 138
aconite 93, 95
Aconitum napellus, 95; *see also* aconite
Alamut 100–1, 107
Albertus Magnus 94
alcohol 8, 30–3, 34, 37, 38, 40, 42, 44, 93, 108, 113, 117, 119, 145
alcoholism 109–11
ale 33
Algonquians 69, 80, 81
Aloeddin (Ala al-Din Muhammad) 100–1
altered states of consciousness 7, 8, 17–19, 22, 28, 30, 53, 54, 59, 62, 64, 76, 83, 85–6, 105, 128, 144, 145, 146
Amahuaca 72
Amanita muscaria 8, 34, 38–40, 46, 49, 69, 72; *see also* fly-agaric
Amazon 8, 18, 53–5, 56–68, 122
American Indians 35, 57, 67, 71, 139, 140
amphetamine(s) 8, 95
Anadenanthera 8, 62, 64; *A. peregrina* 62, 64
Angel Dust 112, 114; *see also* PCP
Anhalonium lewinii 103
Apaches 77
aphrodisiac effects: betel 127; cocoa 123; mandrake 97; opium 27–8
Areca catechu 126; *see also* areca palm
areca palm 126–31
Arnhem Land 111, 136–7
Aryans *see* Indo-Iranians
Assassins 100–2, 107
Athapaskans 69
Atropa belladonna 94; *see also* belladonna
atropine 93, 94, 96
Avesta 43, 45, 47, 50, 51, 52
ayahuasca 57; *see also Banisteriopsis, yajé*
Aztecs 70, 73, 74–5, 123

Bacon, Francis 98
Baden culture 31–2
Bambara 117
Banisteriopsis 8, 53, 55, 56, 57–9; *B. caapi* 57–8; *B. inebrians* 58
barbiturates 108, 122

Bat Cave *see* Cueva de los Murciélagos
Baudelaire, Charles 90, 102–3, 106
Beat movement 106
beer 30, 31, 57
Bell Beakers 32
belladonna 8, 90, 93–4
benzene 111
benzine 8, 109
betel 8, 115, 126–32, 135, 138
Bimin-Kuskusmin 83–9
Bindibu 135
black hellebore *see Helleborus niger*
Bogoras, Waldemar 41, 42
Boletus 82; *Boletus* [*Tubiporus*] 88–9
Borhegyi, Stephen F. de 44, 70
Bourgois, Philippe 113–14
Bourke, Captain John 49, 69
Bradley, Richard 19, 22
Brady, Maggie 109
Brittany 19–24, 28
Bronze Age 24, 25, 26, 29, 31, 39
Brough, John 46
Brunton, Ron 133–4
bruyère 141
Bryonia diocia see bryony
bryony 98–9
Bufo 71–2; *B. agua* 96; *B. marinus* 71–2; *see also* toad
bufotenine 71–2
burial and intoxication 21–3, 25, 32–3, 37, 87, 88, 127, 129
Burroughs, William S. 106–8

cacao 65, 73; *see also* cocoa
cacti 74; *see also* peyote
cafés 10, 121
caffeine 117, 122, 123
Camellia thea 123
cannabis 8, 30, 34, 35–7, 44, 145; *see also* hemp
Cannabis sativa 28, 29, 32; *see also* hemp
cassowary 86, 87, 88, 129
Catha edulis 118
Central Asia 43, 50, 51, 126
Cherokee 80
Chichimecas 75
China/Chinese 43, 46, 50, 123–4, 126
Chinese medicine 50, 124
chloroform 8, 108–9
chocolate 123
Christianity 75, 76, 77–8, 129, 135, 141

Chukchee 39, 41–2
CIA 74
cigarettes 10, 81, 112, 115, 120, 129, 142, 143, 145
cigars 57, 139, 142–3
Clark, A. J. 92, 95
Club des Haschischins, Le 102
Coahuila 75
coca 8, 112–14, 115–16, 118, 138, 144
Coca-Cola 118
cocaine 8, 112–14, 116, 144
cocoa 8, 71, 107, 121; *see also* cacao
Coffea arabica 121
coffee 8, 57, 116, 117, 119, 121–2, 128, 129
cohoba 62, 72; *see also Anadenanthera*
coke *see* cocaine
cola 8, 115, 116–18, 128
Cola acuminata 116; *see also* cola
Cola nitada 116; *see also* cola
Comanche 76
Conium maculatum 95
Conocybe 74
Corded Ware beakers 32
crack 90, 113–14
Crowley, Aleister 102, 104
Cueva de los Murciélagos 25, 28
Cypriot Base-Ring pottery 25–6, 29

Datura 49, 58; *D. stramonium* 102
deadly nightshade *see* belladonna
Decadent movement 102–3
Devil/evil spirit 75, 78, 90, 94, 95, 96, 103, 108
distillation 40
Dobkin de Rios, Marlene 69–73, 76
Dogrib 69
Dowson, Thomas 17–19, 61
Duboisia hopwoodii 137
Duyong Cave 127

Egypt 13, 25, 26–8, 31, 73, 97, 101
Eliade, Mircea 19, 38, 41, 42
élites 33, 77, 115, 120, 129, 134–5, 146
Elizabetha princeps 65
Ellis, Havelock 103–4
Emboden, William 7, 57, 70, 73, 74, 83, 93, 95, 115, 133
entoptic phenomena 18–19, 22, 54, 61, 103–4
Ephedra 44, 45
Er Lannic 23
Erica arborea 141

eroticism and intoxicants 59, 61, 82, 92–3, 100, 109, 117, 127; *see also* aphrodisiacs, phallicism
ether 8, 109
Ethroxylum coca 115; *see also* coca

Fang 96
fermentation 30–1, 44, 72, 123
Flattery, David Stophlet 48, 50–1, 53, 59
flight, sensation of 54–5, 64, 67–8, 90–5
fly-agaric 8, 14, 34, 38–42, 44–9, 52, 69
flying carpet, legend of 55
flying ointments 90–5
Frazer, J. G. 11, 12, 16
Freud, Sigmund 113
frog 61, 69–72, 96, 108; *see also* toad
Furst, Peter 71, 75

Gautier, Théophile 102
Gavrinis 22–4
Gell, Alfred 128–9
Genista canariensis 81
ginger 84, 86, 88, 117
Ginsberg, Allen 106, 107
ginseng 50
Globular Amphorae 31
glue 8, 109
Graves, Robert 16
Greece/Greeks 13, 26, 31, 94
Grewia polygama 136
Grevillea 135
Guaraní 55
Gysin, Brion 106–7

hadith 52
Haida 81
hallucinations 8, 18, 22, 41–2, 51, 53, 55, 57, 61–2, 64, 68, 73, 74, 77, 94, 95, 103–4, 105, 106, 108, 109, 112, 124, 127, 137, 145; auditory 8, 41, 62, 74, 86, 109; visual 8, 18, 41–2, 73, 74, 86, 109, 111
hallucinogens 8, 41, 44, 56, 57, 62, 66–7, 68–79, 82–3, 90, 94, 96, 97, 106, 126, 139
haoma 35, 43, 47, 50–5, 59
harmaline 8, 53
harmel 8, 50–1, 53–5
harmine 53, 59
Hasan-i-Sabbah 101
hashish 44, 45, 49, 90, 101–3, 106, 109, 119; *see also* cannabis, hemp
Heim, Roger 74, 82–3
Heimella 88
Helleborus niger 96
hemlock *see Conium maculatum*
hemp 28–30, 33, 35, 37
henbane 8, 90, 93, 94–5
Hermetic Order of the Golden Dawn 104
Herodotus 35–7
heroin 8, 90, 106, 112, 113, 114, 144
Hochdorf Hallstatt D 30
Hofmann, Albert 74

Hopewell pipes 79–80
Huaca Prieta 65, 67
Huichol 75
Hultkrantz, Åke 76
hunter-gatherers 12–14, 16
Huxley, Aldous 44, 103, 104, 105
hyoscyamine 94, 96
Hyoscyamus niger, 94; *see also* henbane
hypnotics 8, 73, 97

India 43, 48, 49, 50, 123, 127
Indo-Aryans 43, 45, 48
Indo-Iranians 35, 45, 46, 50, 55
India 48, 52
inebriants 8
initiation 59, 83–9, 100, 129, 134, 137
Inquisition 75
International Federation for Internal Freedom 105
Inuit 69, 81
Iran 43, 48–9, 50–1, 53–5
Iron Age 24–5, 30
Ismailis 101

jaguar 54, 62, 66–8
James I 140
Jimson weed *see Datura stramonium*
Jochelson, Waldemar 40, 42
Jones, Sir William 50

Kamchadal 39, 40, 42
Karuk 80
kava 8, 115, 129, 132–5
Kiambi 83
Kiowa 76, 103
Koryak 39, 40–2
koumish 30
Krishna 48
Kuma 82–3

La Barre, Weston 46, 68, 75
laboratory experiments with intoxicants: LSD and mescaline 18, 74; peyote 76; psilocybin(e) 105
Lagochilus inebrians 126
Leary, Timothy 105–6
Lévi-Strauss, Claude 13, 46, 68, 69
levitation, sensation of 64
Lewin, Louis 7, 103, 109, 124, 133
Lewis-Williams, David 17–19, 61
lime 64, 115, 126–30, 138
Lindstrom, Lamont 132, 133
Linnaeus 123, 139
Lobelia 80
Lophophora 74, 103; *L. diffusa* 74; *L. lewinii* 103; *L. williamsii* 74, 103
LSD 8, 18, 74, 105, 106, 109
lycanthropy 66, 90–3

macroscopia 49, 64
mandragora *see* mandrake
Mandragora officinalis 96; *see also* mandrake
Mandragora officinarum Linn. 96; *see also* mandrake

mandrake 8, 50, 73, 93, 96–9
Mansfield, Katherine 104
marihuana 113; *see also* cannabis
Mascagnia psilophylla 58
Maué 68
Mayans 69–73
Mazatecs 74
mead 30, 31, 33
medical effects of intoxicants 102; betal 127; cocaine 113; coffee 122; ginseng 50; harmel 50–1; *Lobelia* 80–1; mandrake 97–9; mushrooms 68; opium 26, 28; PCP 112; qat 118; tea 124, 126; tobacco 140
meditation 7, 124–5, 128, 145
meerschaum 141
megalithic art 19–24
Merrillees, Robert 25, 26, 29
mescal (buttons) 74, 103–4; *see also* peyote
mescaline 8, 18, 74, 103–5
Mexico 44, 57, 65, 68, 71, 74–6, 79, 104, 123
microscopia 49
Mixtecs 74
Moore, James 74
Moreau, Jacques Joseph 101–2
morphine 24, 112
mortars (and pestles) 43, 66, 70, 128
Mountain Ok 82, 83, 89
Muhammad the Prophet 43, 51, 52, 100
mushrooms 8, 38, 41, 44, 45, 46, 57, 68–71, 73–4, 82–3, 87, 88–9; *see also Amanita muscaria*, fly-agaric
mushroom stones 70
myth and intoxicants 40–1, 61, 68

narcotic(s) 7, 8, 24, 62, 97, 118, 145
Native American Church 76
Nelson, Harold 83
Neolithic 12, 13, 19–25, 28–33, 145
Nerval, Gérard de 102
New Guinea 82–9, 128–32, 134, 135–6
Nicol de Villemain, Jean 139
Nicotiana 135, 139; *N. ingulba* 135; *N. rustica* 65, 139; *N. suaveolens* 135; *N. tabacum* 65, 86, 139
nicotine 127, 135, 137
North American Indians 57, 76
Nupe kingdom 118
Nymphaea ampla 73; *Nymphaea caerulea* 73; Nymphaeaceae 73

Oaxaca 74
Ojibway 69
Old Man of the Mountains 99–101, 107
Olmecs 72
ololiuqui 70
Oma river basin 65
opium 8, 24–8, 29, 30, 33, 49, 73, 106, 112, 113, 144, 145
Orinoco 64, 67, 72

Index

Ostyak 39
Otomac 64

Palaeolithic (Upper) 12–19, 22, 59, 106; cave art 13, 14–19
Palaeosiberians 39
Panaeolus 74
Papaver rhoeas 24; *Papaver somniferum* 24, 28; *see also* opium
Parry, Jonathan 48
parsley 93, 95
Patanjali 49
Pazyryk 37
PCP 90, 111–12, 113, 114
Peganum harmala 50, 59
Periploca 44, 45
Persepolis 35
petrol sniffing 109–11
peyote (cactus) 8, 74–9, 103–4
Peyote Religion 78
phallicism 59, 61, 70, 93
phosphenes 18, 54, 61–2; *see also* entoptic phenomena
pipe cups 28–9
Piper 88, 127; *P. betle* 126; *P. methysticum* 132
pipes 79–81, 88, 136–7, 139–42
pituri 8, 136–9
Pliny 26
poison 71–2, 94–6, 97, 103, 109, 126, 138
Pokomam 72
Polo, Marco 99–101
polypod bowls 28–9
Poole, Fitz 83
prayer 7, 118, 124
Prestonia amazonica 58
psilocin(e) 74, 83
Psilocybe 8, 74, 83, 105; *P. caerulescens* var. *nigripes* 74; *P. kumaenorum* 89; *P. mexicana* 74
psilocybin(e) 74, 83, 105
psychedelic/a 14, 90, 103–6
Punk movement 109

qat 8, 115, 118–21

Radin, Paul 77–8
Rave, John 77–9
Reay, Marie 82–3
Reichel-Dolmatoff, Gerardo 18, 54, 59, 60, 62
Rheum palmatum 44
rhubarb 44, 45
Rig Veda 43–7, 50
ritual use of intoxicants 83–9, 144; betel 128–9; coca 112, 116; *haoma/soma* 43, 52–3; hemp 28, 35–6; kava 129, 134–5; mushrooms 69–70; opium 24, 27; peyote 75, 76–7, 103; qat 120;

tobacco 136; yajé 59–61
Rivers, W. H. R. 134
rock art: Amazonian 62; San 19; Shoshonean Coso 19; Siberian 39; *see also* Palaeolithic cave art
Rudenko, S. I. 37
rue 50
Russula 82, 88
Ruta graveolens 50; *see also* rue

sabbat 92–4
Sacy, Silvestre de 101
Sahagún, Bernardino de 73, 75
Salish 69
San Lorenzo (Veracruz) 72
Sandoz Laboratories 74
Sarcostemma 44, 45
Satan 90, 96; *see also* Devil/evil spirit
Schenk, Gustav 72, 94
Schultes, Richard Evans 46, 56, 57, 74, 105, 108
scopolamine 94, 96, 137
Scotch broom *see Genista canariensis*
Scythians 30, 34–7
Selkup 39
shamanism 17, 19, 30, 34, 35, 37–9, 53–4, 56, 58, 59, 61, 64, 65, 66–8, 69, 70, 77, 81, 146
Sherratt, Andrew 23, 29, 33
Shoshoni 19, 76
Siberia/Siberians 14, 34, 37–42, 43, 46, 49, 50, 68
Siegel, Ronald 112
snake 62, 68, 78, 129
snuff 57, 62–8, 72, 139, 141; related artefacts 57, 62–8, 141
Solanaceae 93
Solomon Islands 130, 134
solvents 8, 90, 109–11
soma 43–7, 50, 52, 55
Somalia 118–20
Spanish Harlem 113–14
Spedding, A. L. 116
Spirit Cave 127
Spruce, Richard 57, 67
St Claude 141
stimulants 8, 115, 118–19, 121, 122, 124, 127, 128, 129, 135, 139
Stipa tenacissima 25
Stropharia 74
Stropharia (Psilocybe) cubensis 74
Sundstrom, L. 117
sweat-lodge 35

tea 8, 115, 117, 119, 120, 121, 123–6, 128, 129, 144
telepathine *see* harmine
telepathy 108
Thea sinensis 123
Theobroma cacao 123

Theobroma subinacum 64–5
theobromine 117, 123
Thevet, André 139
Thomson, Donald 135
Thracians 30
toad 69–73, 96
tobacco 8, 38, 42, 57, 59, 65, 69, 79–81, 84, 86–8, 117, 127, 128, 135–43, 144, 145; *see also* cigarettes, cigars, *Nicotiana*, nicotine, pipes, snuff
Toltecs 75
toluene 111
Torres, Constantino Manuel 66
tranquillisers 8
Trobriand Islands 129–30
Tukano 18, 54, 59–62, 66
Tungus 37
Turkestan 118, 125–6

Ugrian peoples 39
urine 40, 45, 47–9, 69

Vacinium uliginosum 40
Vanuatu 132–4
vase-supports 23–4, 28
Virginia 139–41
Virola 8, 64
Vitis sylvestris 31; *Vitis vinifera* 31
vodka 42
Vogul 39
volatile chemicals 81, 109–11

Waika 65
Wasson, R. G. 14, 44–8, 50, 52, 74, 82–3, 105
water-lily 69–70, 73
Watson, Pamela 138
Weitlaner, Roberto J. 74
Wik-mungkan 136
Windfuhr, Gernot 50
wine 30, 31, 33, 37, 57
Winnebago 77
Wiraz, Arda 52–5
witchcraft 14, 55, 73, 90–9, 103
witches' salves *see* flying ointments
Woodlands tradition 79

yajé 53–5, 57–62, 66, 107–8
Yakut 37
Yeats, W. B. 104
Yemen (Republic of) 118, 120
yoga 48, 49
Yurak 41

Zaehner, R. C. 105
Zande 117
Zapotecs 74
Zarathustra 45, 51
Zoroaster *see* Zarathustra
Zoroastrianism 48–9, 52–3, 54